W9-CZO-539

DIRECTORY OF  ILLUSTRATION

SERBIN COMMUNICATIONS, INC.
SANTA BARBARA, CALIFORNIA

PUBLISHER/EDITOR
Glen Robert Serbin

ART DIRECTOR/DESIGN
Mehosh Dziadzio

MANAGING EDITOR
Margie Middleton

ADVERTISING DIRECTOR
John Jimenez

ADVERTISING STAFF
Jason Cohen
Louise Duchein
Bryan Dunn
Lynne Le Couvre
Elizabeth Owen

PRODUCTION COORDINATOR
Karen Hubbard

PRODUCTION STAFF
Elizabeth Owen
Krysia Alisha

EDITORIAL ASSISTANT
Barbara Toohey

ACCOUNTING
Fred Gaeden C.P.A.

BOOKKEEPING
Soans and Associates

GRAPHIC ARTISTS GUILD LIAISON
Paul Basista
Executive Director

COVER DESIGN
Mike McGurl
14 Garbosa Road
Santa Fe, New Mexico 87505
(505) 986-5889

TYPOGRAPHER
The TypeStudio
Tom Buhl

SHIPPING
Corporate Mailing, Inc.
Diversified Mail, Inc.

PRINTER
Dai Nippon, Tokyo

**DISTRIBUTORS TO THE BOOK TRADE
AND ART TRADE IN THE
UNITED STATES AND CANADA BY:**
North Light Books
An Imprint of F&W Publications
1507 Dana Avenue
Cincinnati, Ohio 45207

WORLDWIDE DISTRIBUTION
Hearst Publications International
105 Madison Avenue
New York, NY 10016

The DIRECTORY OF ILLUSTRATION Volume 9 is published by Serbin Communications, Inc., 511 Olive Street, Santa Barbara, California 93101. 805-963-0439. © 1992 by Serbin Communications, Inc., All rights reserved. Copyright under International and Pan-American Copyright Convention. Printed in Japan. ISBN 9628858-1-9.

No part of this book may be reproduced, stored in a retrieval system, or transmitted in any form, or by any means, electronic, mechanical, photocopying, recording or otherwise, without the prior permission of the publisher.

741.6
G76d
n. 9

92-3794
22718428

FROM THE PUBLISHER

FROM THE PUBLISHER

I f you are a buyer of professional illustration, you will find this year's *Directory of Illustration* to be of significant interest. I am proud to announce that the *Directory of Illustration #9* has grown by 60% this year, making the *Directory of Illustration* the fastest growing source book of professional illustration in the world!

Our growth has allowed us to provide you, the buyer of illustration, the most comprehensive *Directory of Illustration* to date. More than 1200 illustrations are published in this year's directory by some of the world's most talented illustrators.

The *Directory of Illustration* is open to both members and non-members of the Graphic Artist Guild. We have provided an Easy Access Index in the front of the book which will allow you to find artists based on subject matter. Because each page represents a small portion of the artists' styles, the Easy Access Index provides additional information not necessarily represented on the artists' pages.

Please remember that the *Directory of Illustration* publishes the original works of our artists and designers. The *Directory of Illustration* is intended as a source for buyers of art to identify and contact the talent appropriate to their needs. It is not intended to be a library of swipe art or stock illustrations. One may be inspired by the work contained in this volume, but using this as the basis for a new design or layout may be considered copyright infringement.

I have the highest respect and appreciation for everyone who worked on the *Directory of Illustration #9*. Special appreciation goes out to my sales team who dedicated four months and 25,000 telephone calls to more than 8,000 illustrators. I would like to thank Paul Basista, Executive Director of the Graphic Artists Guild, for his patience and professional guidance on many concerns related to this project. In addition, I would like to thank Mehosh Dziadzio, Karen Hubbard, Elizabeth Owen and John Jimenez for their special contributions to this year's edition.

I hope you will rely on the *Directory of Illustration* often, and that you will respect the rights of our artists as you would like others to respect your work. The *Directory of Illustration #9* showcases the world's most talented artists. I hope you will take the time to appreciate the creative gifts they possess.

GLEN ROBERT SERBIN
Publisher

ARTICLES OF THE CODE OF FAIR PRACTICE

This code provides the graphic communications industry with an accepted standard of ethics and professional conduct. It presents guidelines for the voluntary conduct of persons in the industry, which may be modified by written agreement between the parties.

ARTICLE 1. Negotiations between an artist* or the artist's representative and a client should be conducted only through an authorized buyer.

ARTICLE 2. Orders or agreements between an artist or artist's representative and buyer should be in writing and shall include the specific rights which are being transferred, the specific fee arrangement agreed to by the parties, delivery date, and a summarized description of the work.

ARTICLE 3. All changes or additions not due to the fault of the artist or artist's representative should be billed to the buyer as an additional and separate charge.

ARTICLE 4. There should be no charges to the buyer for revisions or retakes made necessary by errors on the part of the artist or the artist's representative.

ARTICLE 5. If work commissioned by a buyer is postponed or cancelled, a "kill-fee" should be negotiated based on time allotted, effort expended, and expenses incurred.

ARTICLE 6. Completed work shall be paid for in full and the artwork shall be returned promptly to the artist.

ARTICLE 7. Alterations shall not be made without consulting the artist. Where alterations or retakes are necessary, the artist shall be given the opportunity of making such changes.

ARTICLE 8. The artist shall notify the buyer of any anticipated delay in delivery. Should the artist fail to keep the contract through unreasonable delay or non-conformance with agreed specifications, it will be considered a breach of contract by the artist.

ARTICLE 9. Asking an artist to work on speculation is not deemed professionally reasonable because of its potentially exploitative nature.

ARTICLE 10. There shall be no undisclosed rebates, discounts, gifts, or bonuses requested by or given to buyers by the artist or representative.

ARTICLE 11. Artwork and copyright ownership are vested in the hands of the artist.

ARTICLE 12. Original artwork remains the property of the artist unless it is specifically purchased. It is distinct from the purchase of any reproduction rights.*   *All transactions shall be in writing.

ARTICLE 13. In case of copyright transfers, only specified rights are transferred. All unspecified rights remain vested with the artist.   **All transactions shall be in writing.

ARTICLE 14. Commissioned artwork is not to be considered as "work for hire."

ARTICLE 15. When the price of work is based on limited use and later such work is used more extensively, the artist shall receive additional payment.

Formulated in 1948, revised in 1989
Relations between artist and buyer

4

ARTICLE 16. If exploratory work, comprehensives, or preliminary photographs are bought from an artist with the intention or possibility that another artist will be assigned to do the finished work, this shall be in writing at the time of placing the order.

ARTICLE 18. If no transfer of copyright ownership* has been executed, the publisher of any reproduction of artwork shall publish the artist's copyright notice if the artist so requests at the time of agreement.

ARTICLE 19. The right to remove the artist's name on published artwork is subject to agreement between artist and buyer.

ARTICLE 20. There shall be no plagiarism of any artwork.

ARTICLE 21. If an artist is specifically requested to produce any artwork during unreasonable working hours, fair additional remuneration shall be paid.

ARTICLE 22. All artwork or photography submitted as samples to a buyer should bear the name of the artist or artists responsible for the work. An artist shall not claim authorship of another's work.

ARTICLE 23. All companies and their employees who receive artist portfolios, samples, etc. shall be responsible for the return of the portfolio to the artist in the same condition as received.

ARTICLE 24. An artist entering into an agreement with a representative, studio, or production company for an exclusive representation shall not accept an order from nor permit work to be shown by any other representative or studio. Any agreement which is not intended to be exclusive should set forth the exact restrictions agreed upon between the parties.

ARTICLE 25. No representative should continue to show an artist's samples after the termination of an association.

ARTICLE 26. After termination of an association between artist and representative, the representative should be entitled to a commission for a period of six months on accounts which the representative has secured, unless otherwise specified by contract.

ARTICLE 27. Examples of an artist's work furnished to a representative or submitted to a prospective buyer shall remain the property of the artist, should not be duplicated without the artist's consent, and shall be returned promptly to the artist in good condition.

ARTICLE 28. Contests for commercial purposes are not deemed professionally reasonable because of their potentially speculative and exploitative character.

ARTICLE 29. Interpretation of the Code for the purposes of mediation and arbitration shall be in the hands of the Joint Ethics Committee and is subject to changes and additions at the discretion of the parent organizations through their appointed representatives on the Committee.

Submitting to mediation and arbitration under the auspices of the Joint Ethics Committee is voluntary and requires the consent of all parties to the dispute.

COPYRIGHT 1989 BY THE JOINT ETHICS COMMITTEE, POST OFFICE BOX NUMBER 179, GRAND CENTRAL STATION, NEW YORK, NY 10017.

*THE WORD ARTIST SHOULD BE UNDERSTOOD TO INCLUDE CREATIVE PEOPLE IN THE FIELD OF VISUAL COMMUNICATIONS SUCH AS ILLUSTRATION, GRAPHIC DESIGN, PHOTOGRAPHY, FILM, AND TELEVISION.

**ARTWORK OWNERSHIP, COPYRIGHT OWNERSHIP, AND OWNERSHIP AND RIGHTS TRANSFERS AFTER JANUARY 1, 1978 ARE TO BE IN COMPLIANCE WITH THE FEDERAL COPYRIGHT REVISION ACT OF 1976.

INDEX OF ARTISTS

EASY ACCESS INDEX

The following listings do not necessarily reflect the subjects shown on the artists' pages, but demonstrate the full range of their skills.

ANIMATION

ARCHITECTURAL

BOOK

EASY ACCESS INDEX

EASY ACCESS INDEX

EASY ACCESS INDEX

ON JOINING THE GUILD

When you join the Guild, you're making a very definite statement of your conviction that graphic artists deserve the same respect our society affords other professionals.

JOINING THE GUILD affirms the value of artists working *together* to improve standards of pay and working conditions in our industry. Joining is an endorsement of the highest standards of ethical conduct in the marketplace.

JOINING THE GUILD is joining the effort to advance the rights and interests of artist through legislative reform. Examples: our ongoing fight to end the widespread abuse of the copyright law's "work-for-hire" language; our successful battle against unfair taxation of artists.

JOINING THE GUILD may provide you with a vehicle for contract bargaining — with your employer if you are a staff artist, or even with your client if you are one of a group of free-lance artists regularly working for a given client.

JOINING THE GUILD puts you in contact with other artists who share your concerns. It's a way to share ideas, information, and business skills with your colleagues.

JOINING THE GUILD has immediate practical benefits.

. . .

☆ Members receive the latest edition of the *Graphic Artists Guild Handbook, Pricing & Ethical Guidelines*. This best-seller contains a wealth of information about pricing and trade practices in every corner of the graphic arts. Many consider it an industry "Bible."

☆ Group Health Insurance as well as disability and retirement plans are available to members at favorable rates.

☆ Members receive a subscription to national and local chapter newsletters.

☆ Your local chapter may provide direct marketing assistance through job referral services, trade shows and other activities.

☆ Members receive substantial discounts on supplies from many dealers, and on page-rates in many illustration and design directories.

☆ Chapters also run "hotlines" to give members access to advice and referrals to Guild-approved lawyers and accountants should you need them.

☆ Chapters produce educational programs and social events for members.

. . .

The Graphic Artists Guild is the only organization of its kind in the United States. If you want to work together with other artists to effect positive change in the status of artists in the marketplace and in society, YOU BELONG IN THE GUILD!

PLEASE PHOTOCOPY THIS PAGE, FILL OUT ALL PORTIONS OF THIS FORM AND MAIL IT WITH YOUR DUES PAYMENT AND INITIATION FEE TO:

MEMBERSHIP STATUS

Guild Membership comprises two categories: Member and Associate Member. Only working graphic artists are eligible to become full Members. Interested People in related fields who support the goals and purposes of the Guild are welcome to join as Associate Members, as are graphic arts students and retired artists. Associate Members may participate in all Guild activities and programs, but not hold office or vote.

○ I earn more than half of my income from my own graphic work, and am therefore eligible to join the Guild as a Member.

○ I wish to join the Guild as an Associate Member.

The Graphic Artists Guild is a national organization with local chapters. Membership applications are processed at the national office; you'll be enrolled either in a local chapter serving your area or in the "At-Large" chapter if there is no local chapter near you.

**GRAPHIC ARTISTS GUILD
11 WEST 20TH STREET, 8TH FLOOR
NEW YORK, NY 10011-3704**

NAME

ADDRESS

CITY   STATE   ZIP

BUSINESS PHONE   HOME PHONE

DISCIPLINE(S)

Please mark "1" for the area in which you do most of your work, and "2" and "3" for additional specialties.

● GRAPHIC DESIGN
● ILLUSTRATION
● PRE-PRODUCTION ART
● SURFACE DESIGN
● CARTOONING
● PHOTOGRAPHY
● COMPUTER ARTS
● PRODUCTION/MECHANICALS
● ART DIRECTION
● ARTISTS' REPRESENTATIVE
● TEACHING PROFESSIONAL
● VIDEO/BROADCAST DESIGN
● OTHER _____
  _____

MEMBERSHIP STATEMENT

Please read and sign the following:

I derive more income from my own work as a graphic artist than I do from the owner or manager of any business which profits from the buying and/or selling of graphic artwork.*

I, the undersigned, agree to abide by the Constitution of the Graphic Artists Guild and do hereby authorize the Guild to act as my representative with regard to negotiation of agreements approved by the Guild membership to improve pricing and ethical standards of the graphic arts profession.**

I further understand that my membership in the Graphic Artists Guild is continuous and that I will be billed for membership dues annually on the anniversary of my original application. If I wish to resign from the Graphic Artists Guild, I understand that I must resign in writing, and that I will be responsible for the payment of any dues owned prior to the date of my resignation.

*This statement does not apply to associate members.

**Your membership package will contain a copy of the constitution. To obtain one prior to joining, send $1 with your request to the national office. The document is also on file at national and chapter offices for inspection.

SIGNATURE   DATE

DUES AND INITIATION FEE

To offset the administrative expense of processing new memberships, the Guild collects a $25. one-time fee with membership application. ■ Guild dues depend upon membership category and income level. Income level refers to your total adjusted gross income from your federal tax return.

Member Dues (Please Check Category):
☐ Income under $12,000/yr ... $100 per year
☐ Income $12,000-30,000/yr .. $135 per year
☐ Income over $30,000/yr ...... $175 per year

Associate Member Dues:
☐ Students .... $55 per year
☐ Others .... $95 per year

Method of Payment
☐ Check   ☐ Money Order

Dues* _____
Initiation Fee $25
Total enclosed _____

*You may remit one-half of your dues with this application (plus the initiation fee), we will bill you for the second half, which must be paid within 120 days.

Returned checks are subject to $10 service charge. On occasion, the Guild allows the use of its mailing list by companies selling products of interest to our members. Please check this box if you do not wish to have your name made available in this manner. ☐

EMPLOYMENT STATUS

If you are on staff and do freelance work as well, please mark "1" for staff and "2" for freelance.

○ STAFF   ○ RETIRED GRAPHIC ARTIST

○ FREELANCE (includes business owners, partners, and corporation principals)

○ STUDENT

School _____

Year of graduation _____
(Students must include a photocopy of current college I.D.)

For office use only: PEGS_____ MEMBERSHIP CARD_____ AZW_____

The Guild's First 25 Years

This year marks the 25th anniversary of the Graphic Artists Guild. An historic milestone, the Guild's Silver Anniversary is cause for celebration—not only for what we've accomplished over the years, but also for new undertakings, like the *Eye to Eye* conference held earlier this year, that signify the Guild's growth and importance in the industry.

Foremost among the Guild's accomplishments is the publication of the *Graphic Artists Guild Handbook, Pricing & Ethical Guidelines*. A third printing of the current 7th edition, originally released in May, 1991, was completed early in 1992 and an unprecedented fourth printing is planned for early in 1993. With more than 52,000 copies already in print, this best seller is clearly the industry's primary reference for pricing guidelines and professional standards and practices.

Noted illustrator Marshall Arisman (Guild member since 1982), said that if the *Guild Handbook, Pricing & Ethical Guidelines* were the only thing the Guild ever accomplished, that alone would justify our existence. But in highlighting Guild activities since 1967, a noteworthy record is revealed:

1967   Guild organized in Detroit with initial membership of 113.

1971   New York Chapter chartered.

1973   First edition of *Graphic Artists Guild Handbook, Pricing & Ethical Guidelines* published as a 20-page booklet.

Favorable decision obtained from Copyright Royalty Tribunal which raises fees and improves reporting procedures for 260 PBS stations regarding use of previously published art for broadcasting.

1975   Formation of Professional Practices Committee to assist Guild members in resolution of disputes.

Second edition of *Graphic Artists Guild Handbook, Pricing & Ethical Guidelines* published as a 40-page booklet.

1976   First publication of talent *Directory*, the first source book serving the needs of illustrators.

Illustrators Guild merges with Graphic Artists Guild.

1977   New York Chapter co-sponsors the independent Joint Ethics Committee to promote the industry's oldest ethical practices code and to provide mediation and arbitration for industry practitioners.

1978   Independent national Guild office organized; first national board and officers elected in 1979 and first national convention occurs in 1980.

Atlanta chapter chartered

1979   Third edition of *Graphic Artists Guild Handbook, Pricing & Ethical Guidelines* published as a 48-page booklet.

Textile Designers Guild merges with Graphic Artists Guild.

Long-term legislative drive initiated which targets federal copyright and tax laws and promotes model legislation to establish legal rights for artists at federal and state levels.

Model business forms drafted for various graphic art disciplines.

Negotiation with several publishers results in their withdrawing work-for-hire contracts.

1980   Boston chapter chartered. Favorable ruling from IRS provides Guild with non-profit status as a "labor organization" which allows flexibility and broader activities as a professional association beyond those of purely "educational" or "philanthropic" associations.

1981   Professional Education Program started by New York Chapter.

Oregon passes an "artists' fair practices" law (Sects. 359.350-359.365 of Rev. Stat.) based on Guild's model law.

1982   Indianapolis Chapter chartered.

Fourth edition of *Graphic Artists Guild Handbook, Pricing & Ethical Guidelines* published as a 136-page book.

Guild succeeds in passage of state's "artists' fair practices" law (Sect. 988 of Civil Code).

Assistance provided in the formation of the National Writers Union.

Responding to Guild opposition, IRS withdraws proposed rule that would have disallowed a home-studio deduction where artist has a primary source of income at another location and from other type of work.

Guild forms coalition of creators' groups including photographers and writers, to lobby for work-for-hire reform in U.S. Congress. Forty-two organizations join coalition efforts, the largest creators' advocacy coalition in history.

Graphic Artists Guild Foundation organized, receives NEA grant for study.

New York Chapter succeeds in passage of state's "artists' fair practices" law (Sects. 1401 & 1403 of Arts & Cult. Aff. Law) and "Artists' Authorship Rights" law (Art. 12-J of Gen. Bus. Law).

1983   Vermont Chapter chartered.

1984   Cartoonist Guild merges with Graphic Artists Guild.

Fifth edition of *Graphic Artists Guild Handbook, Pricing & Ethical Guidelines* published as a 194-page book.

Testimony is presented before the Democratic National Platform Committee on professional issues.

Proposed "Copyright Justice Act" to reform work-for-hire provision of the Copyright Law by eliminating instances in which artists lose rights and benefits as creators of their work.

1985   Contract terms renegotiated with Children's Television Workshop.

Guild Foundation drafts ethical guidelines for contests and competitions and forms Giolito Communications Center, a specialized reference library.

Boston Chapter succeeds in passage of state's "Arts Preservation Act."

National legal referral network established.

1986   Testimony before Congressional Office of Technology Assessment regarding impact of technology on the profession.

Central Florida Chapter chartered.

1987   At-Large Chapter organized to provide unaffiliated members with representation on national board.

Sixth edition of *Graphic Artists Guild Handbook, Pricing & Ethical Guidelines* published as a 208-page book.

1988   Albany Chapter chartered

Guild spearheads formation of "Artists For Tax Equity" (AFTE) coalition to confront intended application of "uniform tax capitalization" requirements on all artists and designers. Coalition grows to 75 organizations representing nearly one million artists and designers.

Volume 5 of the Guild's *Directory of Illustration* released in large, 9″ x 12″ format and is published annually.

1989   Guild's leadership helps "Artists For Tax Equity" win necessary exemption from "uniform tax capitalization" for all artists and graphic designers.

Guild, through the Copyright Justice Coalition, helps convince the Supreme Court to decide in favor of sculptor James Earl Reid in the landmark decision which virtually ends work-for-hire for freelancers in the absence of a written agreement.

Guild presents testimony on work-for-hire abuses to Senate Judiciary's Subcommittee on Patents, Copyrights and Trademarks.

1990   Atlanta Chapter helps win protection for artists in Georgia, requiring printers to obtain written authorization of copyright clearance for all print orders over $1,000.

Guild, together with the AIGA and the SEGD begin working to clarify sales tax collection guidelines for illustrators and graphic designers in New York state.

1991   Expanded and updated seventh edition of *Graphic Artists Guild Handbook, Pricing & Ethical Guidelines* published as a 240-page book. Three printings have been completed, bringing the total number of copies in circulation over 52,000.

Guild takes leadership role to address health care crisis for artists and designers, formally endorses universal health legislation in Congress. Steps are taken to organize "Artists United for Universal Health," a coalition of arts and artists organizations dedicated to this goal.

1992   Guidelines for the Interpretation of Sales Tax-Requirements for Graphic Designers and Illustrators, formulated by Guild, AIGA and SEGD are approved by New York State Department of Taxation.

Guild organizes *Eye to Eye*, its first national conference and trade show, celebrating 25 years of advancing the interests of creators.

The Guild's Silver Anniversary is certainly cause for celebration, but it's also a stepping stone to a golden future for the organization, its members and the industry.

Copyright 1987 Volker E.H. Antoni (Revisions by Paul Basista, 1992, made with author's permission).

THE GUILD'S  BOOKSHELF

**Graphic Artists Guild Handbook,
Pricing & Ethical Guidelines
7th Edition**
240 pp., $22.95
An indispensable reference for artists and
buyers. Contains the results of a survey of
pricing levels in every branch of the
graphic arts plus information on estimates,
proposals, contracts, copyrights, and other
aspects of the business relationship
between artist and buyer.

**The Artists Complete Health &
Safety Guide**
by Monona Rossol. 238 pp., $16.95
Covers everything you need to know
about art materials to make your workplace
safe in compliance with USA and Canada
right-to-know laws.

**Business & Legal Forms for
Graphic Designers**
by Tad Crawford & Eva Doman Bruck.
208 pp., $19.95
These two success kits for illustrators and
graphic designers provide complete sets of
business and legal forms, sample contracts
and a wealth of information to meet your
every need as a creative professional.

**Disk Version–Business & Legal Forms for
Graphic Designers.**
Contains the forms only. You must have PageMaker
and specify MAC or IBM. $14.95

Business & Legal Forms for Illustrators
by Tad Crawford. 160 pp., $15.95
The success kit for Illustrators. A complete set of
business and legal forms, including sample
contracts.

How to Sell Your Photographs & Illustrations
by Elliott & Barbara Gordon. 128 pp., $16.95
Who buys your work? How should you reach these
buyers, set up your portfolio, price your work and
get a favorable contract? Guidelines are laid out to
show what you need for success in these two
challenging fields.

Legal Guide for the Visual Artist
by Tad Crawford. 224 pp., $18.95
Revised and expanded, this highly acclaimed guide
covers copyright and moral laws, studio leases,
selling reproduction rights, model contracts, and
valuable resources for the professional.

Licensing Art & Design
by Caryn R. Leland. 112 pp., $12.95
A guide for understanding and negotiating licenses
and royalty agreements. Caryn Leland shows you
how to transform your ideas and images into
profitable ventures.

Make it Legal
by Lee Wilson. 272 pp., $18.95
A guide to copyright, trademark, libel and
false advertising law; privacy and publicity
rights and information needed to protect
yourself and your clients.

Caring For Your Art
by Jill Snyder, with illustrations by Joseph
Montague. 176 pp., $14.95
This book offers step-by-step guidance for
the safekeeping of your artwork with the
best methods to store, handle, document,
photograph, pack, transport, insure and
secure your art.

**Protecting Your Rights and Increasing
Your Income**
by Tad Crawford. $12.95
This 60 minute audio-cassette covers the
basics of copyright law.

The Business of Being an Artist
by Daniel Grant. 224 pp., $16.95
Coverage includes how to get an exhibit,
finding a dealer, contracts, selling work,
using agents, publicists and reps. Education
and work choices, health and safety issues,
and how to obtain grants and commissions.

Fill out order form completely and mail with full payment to:
Graphic Artists Guild, ATTN: Publications, 11 West 20th Street, 8Fl, New York, NY 10011-3704

For credit card orders call 1-212-463-7730 or FAX this form to: 1-212-463-8779. Ask for Guild membership information.

TITLE	UNIT PRICE	QTY	TOTAL
Pricing & Ethical Guidelines 7th Edition	$22.95		
The Artists Complete Health & Safety Guide	$16.95		
Business & Legal Forms for Graphic Designers	$19.95		
Disk Version Business & Legal Forms for Graphic Designers ❑ MAC ❑ IBM	$14.95		
Business & Legal Forms for Illustrators	$15.95		
How to Sell Your Photographs & Illustrations	$16.95		
Legal Guide for the Visual Artist	$18.95		
Licensing Art & Design	$12.95		
Make it Legal	$18.95		
Caring for Your Art	$14.95		
Protecting Your Rights and Increasing Your Income	$12.95		
The Business of Being an Artist	$16.95		
	SUB-TOTAL		
	GUILD MEMBER 15% DISCOUNT		
	SHIPPING & HANDLING		
	SALES TAX		
	TOTAL		

NAME

ADDRESS

CITY   STATE   ZIP

TELEPHONE (HOME)   (BUSINESS)

MC/VISA#   EXP. DATE

SIGNATURE

New York residents add 8.25% state sales tax.
USPS—$3.50 for 1st item/Add $1 for each additional item
UPS—$4.75 for 1st item/Add $1.25 for each additional item

When was the last time you used a visual that was good for 10,000 years.

Over the past ten thousand years human expression has taken many different forms. But so far only the illustration has proven its power to communicate over this entire span of recorded history. So next time use an illustration. Your work may not only survive long after you've left the business, it may survive long after you've left the planet.

ILLUSTRATION.
The Original Visual.

This ad is sponsored by the Graphic Artists Guild.

Arnie Arlow, Creative/Art Director. David Warren, Copywriter. Illustration: The Bettmann Archive.

CLIENTS INCLUDE: ABC-TV·AC&R·AT&T·ACTIFED·AMERICAN EXPRESS·ARISTA·AVON·BACKER SPIEL... OGE... ·BATES·BLOOMINGDALE'S·BULLOCKS·CBS·CLAIROL· COACH· ·COPPERTONE·

BERNARD MAISNER • The "Zelig" of Hand-Lettering.

BERNARD MAISNER HAND LETTERING

Represented by
GERALD & CULLEN RAPP, INC.
108 East 35 St. ◇ New York 10016
(212) 889-3337 • Fax (212) 889-3341

THE FINEST HAND LETTERING · SINCE 1971

ARLEN & SHERRI SCHUMER

The **DYNAMIC DUO** ®

COMIC ART FOR ADVERTISING & EDITORIAL

ace ILLUSTRATION

EST. 1984

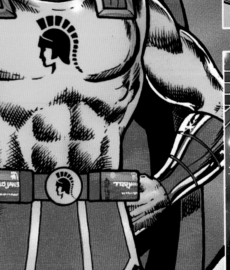

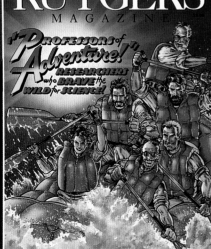

REPRESENTED BY

GERALD & CULLEN RAPP, INC.

108 East 35 St.
New York 10016
Phone: (212) 889-3337
Fax: (212) 889-3341

GERALD & CULLEN RAPP, INC.

108 East 35 St.
New York 10016
Phone: (212) 889-3337
Fax: (212) 889-3341

Jack Davis

108 East 35 St.
New York 10016
Phone: (212) 889-3337
Fax: (212) 889-3341

GERALD & CULLEN RAPP, INC.

Hal Mayforth

DUMPTRUCKS in Reverse

My CAREER

THE CLIENT HAS A FEW PROBLEMS WITH THE SKETCHES. FIRST, THE SHAPE OF THE TOILET BOWL, THAT'S A RESIDENTIAL TOILET, NOT A PUBLIC TOILET. AND AL- SO REMOVE ALL THE BREASTS FROM ALL THE WOMEN. OTHER THAN THAT, IT LOOKS GREAT!

HAS COME TO THIS!!

ALTHOUGH THE CAR YOU RESERVED WAS MISTAKENLY RENTED, THE AGENT ASSURED YOU A REPLACEMENT WILL BE ALONG ANY DAY NOW.

HOW TO AVOID
Cars Rental AGONY

At American International Rent A Car, don't expect to confront empty lots or blank stares. You see, we feel that if you keep the customer happy, you keep the customer. That's why our cars are constantly updated. Our employees are hired for friendliness as well as aptitude. And our prices are more than merely "fair." At American International, we know what you want.

New Yorker Fifth Avenue. We rent quality built Chrysler Corporation products and other fine cars.

AMERICAN INTERNATIONAL RENT A CAR
1-800-527-0202

Wow! WHERE DID THESE CANS COME FROM?

¡HOLA, DUDES! I'M HECTOR AND I'M FROM BARCELONA. Match EACH RADICAL CAN TO THE NAME OF THE COUNTRY IT'S FROM. (THE ANSWERS ARE AT THE BOTTOM OF THE PAGE.) JUST FOR FUN, CHECK OUT THE OLYMPIC GAMES POSTER AND SEE WHICH COUNTRIES HAVE HOSTED THE OLYMPIC SUMMER GAMES.

1. MOROCCO
2. KOREA
3. U.S.A.
4. ITALY
5. CHINA
6. EGYPT
7. THAILAND
8. RUSSIA

© 1992 THE COCA-COLA COMPANY. "COCA-COLA" AND THE DYNAMIC RIBBON DEVICE ARE REGISTERED TRADEMARKS OF THE COCA-COLA COMPANY.

108 East 35 St.
New York 10016
Phone: (212) 889-3337
Fax: (212) 889-3341

GERALD & CULLEN RAPP, INC.

Emmanuel Amit

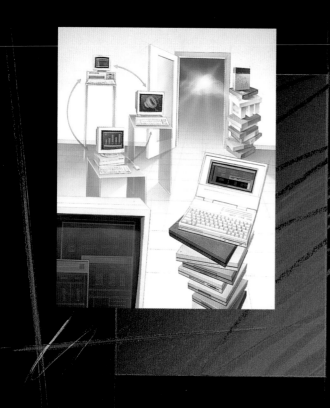

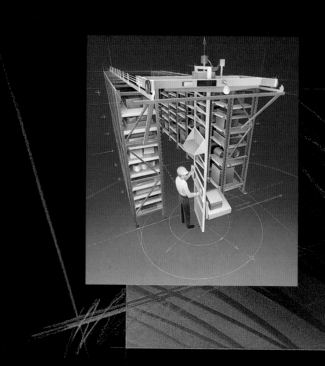

SPIECE GRAPHICS

New Stuff

Dick & Bettejune

Pictures on every Page

The Secret PRISM

Racing Classics

PACIFIC CLIPPER
T·Y·P·E

Mingo Gothic

ABCDEFGHIJKLM
NOPQRSTUVWXYZ
abcdefghijklmno
pqrstuvwxyz123
4567890!.,"$%&

FONTHAUS EXCLUSIVE

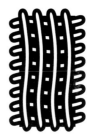

Tweed

ABCDEFGHIJ
KLMNOPQRSTU
VWXYZabcdef
ghijklmnopqrstu
vwxyz12345678
90!.,"$%&?™£¢

FONTHAUS EXCLUSIVE

© 1992 Spiece Graphics

HAND LETTERING & DESIGN

Jim Spiece at the Mac · Spiece Graphics · PO Box 9115 · 1811 Woodhaven #7 · Ft. Wayne, IN 46899
Fax in Studio · Logos & Type Design for Advertising and Editorial · Member Graphic Artists Guild · 219-747-3916

BASEMAN

THE EAST
GERALD RAPP 212.889.3337

EDITORIAL CALLS
718.499.9358

IN THE WEST
JAN COLLIER 415.383.9026

26

BASEMAN

IN THE EAST
GERALD RAPP 212.889.3337

EDITORIAL CALLS
718.499.9358

IN THE WEST
JAN COLLIER 415.383.9026

Fran Seigel
Representing

Kinuko Y. Craft

Fran Seigel   515 Madison Ave., Rm. 2200   New York, NY 10022   (212) 486-9644   Fax (212) 486-9646

Simon & Schuster

Fran Seigel Representing Kinuko Y. Craft

© Playboy 1991

Wines of Spain

Fran Seigel   515 Madison Ave., Rm. 2200   New York, NY 10022   (212) 486-9644   Fax (212) 486-9646

Fran Seigel
Representing John Dawson

Loomis & Toles Artists Materials

Fran Seigel   515 Madison Ave., Rm. 2200   New York, NY 10022   (212) 486-9644   Fax (212) 486-9646

Fran Seigel
Representing John Dawson

Ballantine Books

Fran Seigel   515 Madison Ave., Rm. 2200   New York, NY 10022   (212) 486-9644   Fax (212) 486-9646

Fran Seigel
Representing
Catherine Deeter

Bantam Books

Fran Seigel   515 Madison Ave., Rm. 2200   New York, NY 10022   (212) 486-9644   Fax (212) 486-9646

The C. R. Gibson Company

© Oregon, Wash. & Calif. Pear Bureau 1992 (outdoor board)

Fran Seigel   515 Madison Ave., Rm. 2200   New York, NY 10022   (212) 486-9644   Fax (212) 486-9646

Macmillan Publishing

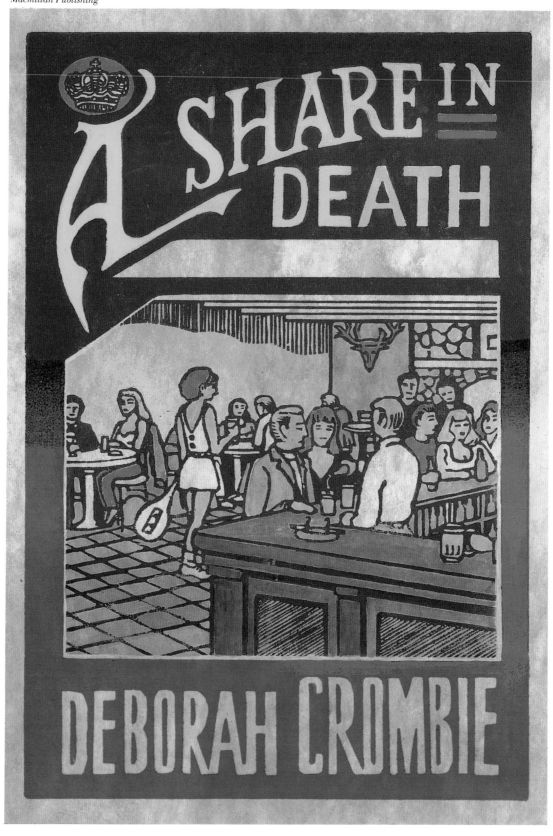

Fran Seigel   515 Madison Ave., Rm. 2200   New York, NY 10022   (212) 486-9644   Fax (212) 486-9646

Fran Seigel   515 Madison Ave., Rm. 2200   New York, NY 10022   (212) 486-9644   Fax (212) 486-9646

Fran Seigel Representing	Earl Keleny

Fran Seigel   515 Madison Ave., Rm. 2200   New York, NY 10022   (212) 486-9644   Fax (212) 486-9646

Amiga World

36

Kiplingers Personal Finance

American Banker

Cleveland Plain Dealer

N. W. Mutual Life Insurance

General Motors/Impact (electric car)

Fran Seigel   515 Madison Ave., Rm. 2200   New York, NY 10022   (212) 486-9644   Fax (212) 486-9646

Connecticut Magazine

Scott Foresman

Fran Seigel   515 Madison Ave., Rm. 2200   New York, NY 10022   (212) 486-9644   Fax (212) 486-9646

C. MICHAEL DUDASH

ARTISTS ASSOCIATES

BILL ERLACHER   212-755-1365
NICOLE EDELL   FAX-755-1987
211 EAST 51ST STREET
NEW YORK, NY 10022

Lu MATTHEWS

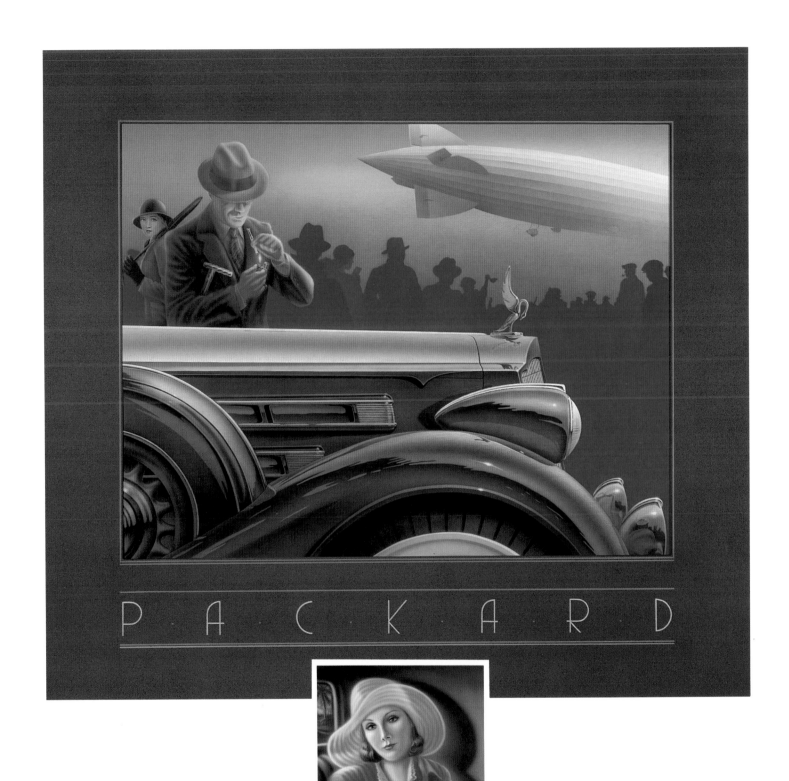

PACKARD

280 MADISON AVE, NEW YORK, NY 10016    IRMELI HOLMBERG   TEL 212 545 9155 • FAX 212 545 9462

Leonid
MYSAKOV

280 MADISON AVE, NEW YORK, NY 10016

IRMELI
HOLMBERG

TEL 212 545 9155 • FAX 212 545 9462

JUDY

PEDERSEN

203 672 2471

280 MADISON AVE, NEW YORK, NY 10016 IRMELI HOLMBERG TEL 212 545 9155 • FAX 212 545 9462

43

Alexandra
W E E M S

280 MADISON AVE, NEW YORK, NY 10016

IRMELI HOLMBERG

TEL 212 545 9155 • FAX 212 545 9462

ALEXANDER

BARSKY

 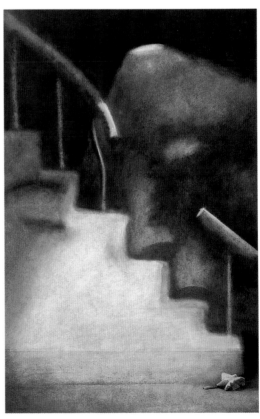

280 MADISON AVE, NEW YORK, NY 10 016      TEL 212 545 9155 • FAX 212 545 9462

45

STUDIO

BRIDY/KELLY

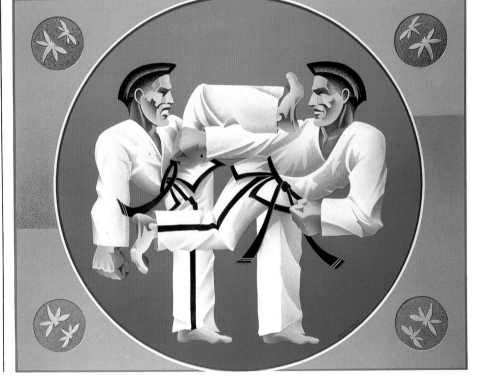

280 MADISON AVE, NEW YORK, NY 10016

IRMELI HOLMBERG

TEL 212 545 9155 • FAX 212 545 9462

46

ISTVAN BANYAI

280 MADISON AVE, NEW YORK, NY 10016   IRMELI HOLMBERG   TEL 212 545 9155 • FAX 212 545 9462

K A R E N

P R I T C H E T T

280 MADISON AVE, NEW YORK, NY 10016   **IRMELI HOLMBERG**   TEL 212 545 9155 • FAX 212 545 9462

B O B
R A D I G A N

280 MADISON AVE, NEW YORK, NY 10016

IRMELI
HOLMBERG

TEL 212 545 9155 • FAX 212 545 9462

49

MOBIL

PARK NICOLLET HEALTH CENTER

BUSINESS WEEK

THE NEWBORN GROUP
ARTIST REPRESENTATIVES: JOAN SIGMAN - MARK HESS
135 EAST 54TH STREET, NEW YORK, NY 10022
(212) 421-0050   FAX (212) 421-0444

50

STUDIO: 576 WESTMINSTER AVE. ELIZABETH NJ 07208 (908) 351-4227 FAX (908) 355-0179

UNITED NATIONS POSTAL SERVICE

GRAND MARNIER USA

ST. LOUIS ZOO

U.N.E.P.

THE NEWBORN GROUP
ARTIST REPRESENTATIVES: JOAN SIGMAN - MARK HESS
135 EAST 54TH STREET, NEW YORK, NY 10022
(212) 421-0050   FAX (212) 421-0444

51

CENTEL CORPORATION

AGENA BUSINESS SYSTEMS

THE WORLD MONITOR

THE NEWBORN GROUP

ARTIST REPRESENTATIVES: JOAN SIGMAN - MARK HESS
135 EAST 54TH STREET, NEW YORK, NY 10022
(212) 421-0050   FAX (212) 421-0444

STUDIO: 471   FIFTH   STREET   BROOKLYN   NY   11215   (718)   768-7367

SAN FRANCISCO FOCUS

POCKETBOOKS

GROVE PRESS

7 DAYS

METAPHOR COMPUTER

THE NEWBORN GROUP

ARTIST REPRESENTATIVES: JOAN SIGMAN - MARK HESS
135 EAST 54TH STREET, NEW YORK, NY 10022
(212) 421-0050 FAX (212) 421-0444

53

STUDIO: 552 BROADWAY 3RD FLOOR NEW YORK NY 10012 TEL & FAX (212) 274-1705

INDUSTRY WEEK

IBM

AMD

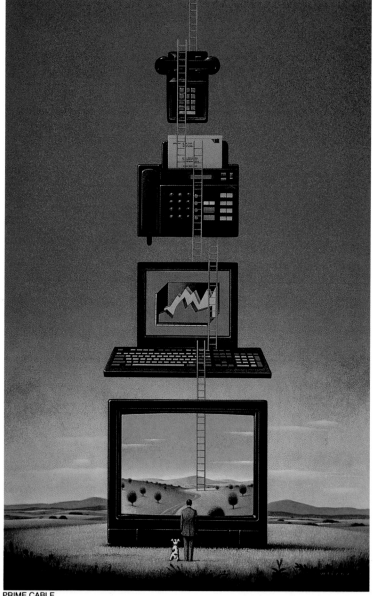

PRIME CABLE

THE NEWBORN GROUP
ARTIST REPRESENTATIVES: JOAN SIGMAN - MARK HESS
135 EAST 54TH STREET, NEW YORK, NY 10022
(212) 421-0050   FAX (212) 421-0444

STUDIO: 5955   SAWMILL   RD.   DOYLESTOWN   PA   18901   TEL   &   FAX   (215)   297-0849

TERESA FASOLINO

WESTINGHOUSE

SKANE HARVEST FESTIVAL

WORKMAN PUBLISHING

ROYAL VIKING

THE NEWBORN GROUP
ARTIST REPRESENTATIVES: JOAN SIGMAN - MARK HESS
135 EAST 54TH STREET, NEW YORK, NY 10022
(212) 421-0050 FAX (212) 421-0444

55

SCHOLASTIC

THE NEWBORN GROUP

ARTIST REPRESENTATIVES: JOAN SIGMAN - MARK HESS
135 EAST 54TH STREET, NEW YORK, NY 10022
(212) 421-0050 FAX (212) 421-0444

STUDIO: BOX 325 RT. 28 RESERVOIR RD. SHOKAN NY 12481 (914) 657-6024 FAX (914) 657-6114

WARNER BOOKS

MASTERCARD

NEWSWEEK

FORBES FYI

THE NEWBORN GROUP

ARTIST REPRESENTATIVES: JOAN SIGMAN - MARK HESS
135 EAST 54TH STREET, NEW YORK, NY 10022
(212) 421-0050   FAX (212) 421-0444

57

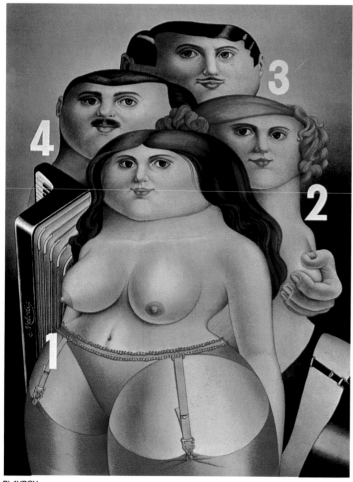

PLAYBOY

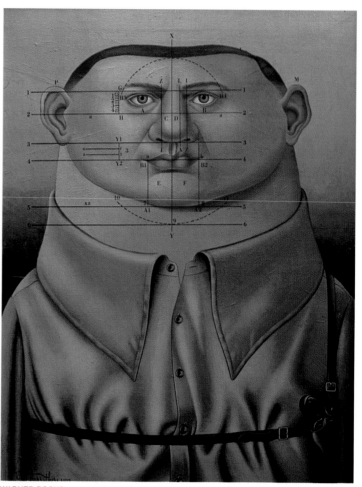

WARNER BOOKS

NYNEX

OUI MAGAZINE

THE NEWBORN GROUP
ARTIST REPRESENTATIVES: JOAN SIGMAN-MARK HESS
135 EAST 54TH STREET, NEW YORK, NY 10022
(212) 421-0050 FAX (212) 421-0444

STUDIO: 270 FIFTH STREET #1B BROOKLYN NY 11215 (718) 965-1330

ROBERT GIUSTI

GENERAL ELECTRIC/AUDUBON

AIR CANADA

PIRELLI

THE NEWBORN GROUP
ARTIST REPRESENTATIVES: JOAN SIGMAN - MARK HESS
135 EAST 54TH STREET, NEW YORK, NY 10022
(212) 421-0050 FAX (212) 421-0444

59

Reynold Ruffins

51 HAMPTON STREET
SAG HARBOR, NY 11963

(516) 725-3480

Reynold Ruffins

51 Hampton Street
Sag Harbor, NY 11963

(516) 725-3480

HARPERCOLLINS

HARPERCOLLINS

WENDELL MINOR · 15 OLD NORTH ROAD · P.O.B. 1135 · WASHINGTON, CT · 06793 · 203 868-9101 · FAX 868-9512

US POSTAL SERVICE

SIMON AND SCHUSTER INC.

MBI, INC.

WENDELL MINOR · 15 OLD NORTH ROAD · P.O.B. 1135 · WASHINGTON, CT · 06793 · 203 868-9101 · FAX 868-9512

Meg Akiyama
2330 Schoolside Avenue
Monterey Park, CA 91754

(818) 584-4137

Member of The Society of Illustrators,
Los Angeles

64

Nancy Barnet

8928 Shady Vista Court
Elk Grove, CA 95624

Tele/Fax (916) 685-4147

Member:
Graphic Artists Guild
Sacramento Illustrators Guild
Society of Children's Book Writers
Colored Pencil Society of America

WILSON McLEAN

902 BROADWAY, SUITE 1603 NEW YORK, N.Y. 10010   (212) 473-5554

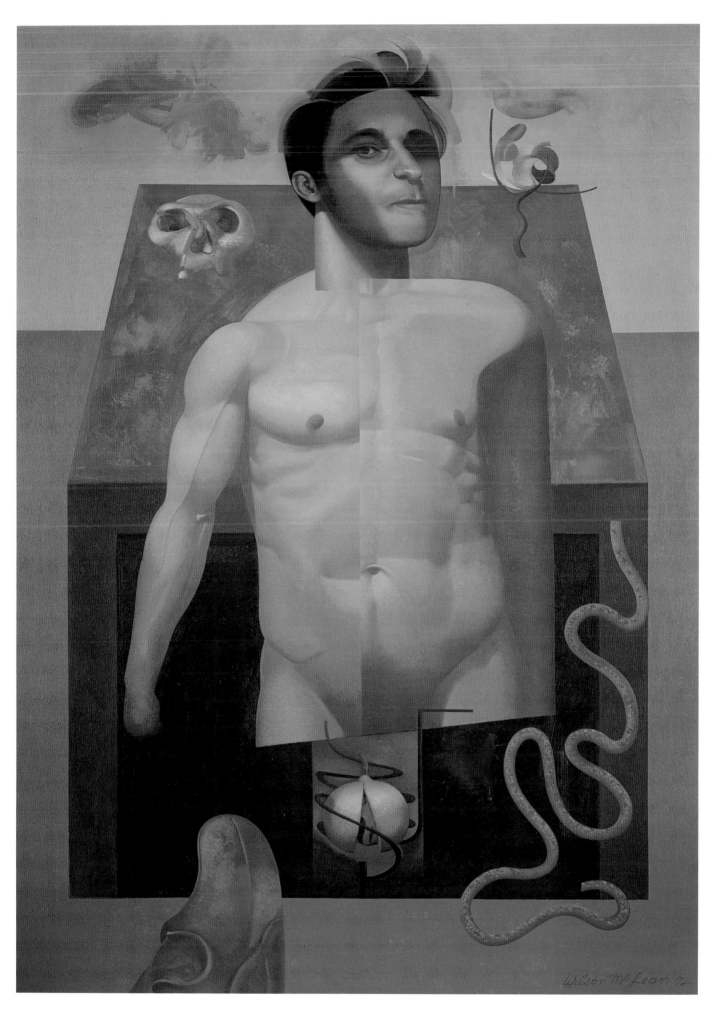

WILSON McLEAN
902 BROADWAY, SUITE 1603 NEW YORK, N.Y. 10010   (212) 473-5554

CLIFF→KNECHT

ARTIST REPRESENTATIVE

309 WALNUT ROAD PITTSBURGH, PA 15202   PHONE 412 • 761 • 5666 FAX 412 • 261 • 3712

CLIFF‣KNECHT
ARTIST REPRESENTATIVE

309 WALNUT ROAD PITTSBURGH, PA 15202 PHONE 412 • 761 • 5666 FAX 412 • 261 • 3712

©1992 THE WALT DISNEY COMPANY

©1992 THE WALT DISNEY COMPANY

CLIFF→KNECHT

ARTIST REPRESENTATIVE

309 WALNUT ROAD PITTSBURGH, PA 15202   PHONE 412 • 761 • 5666 FAX 412 • 261 • 3712

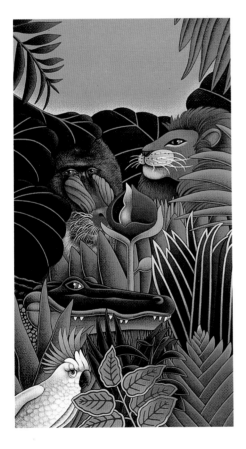

CLIFF KNECHT
ARTIST REPRESENTATIVE

309 WALNUT ROAD PITTSBURGH, PA 15202   PHONE 412 • 761 • 5666 FAX 412 • 261 • 3712

CLIFF·KNECHT
ARTIST REPRESENTATIVE

309 WALNUT ROAD PITTSBURGH, PA 15202 PHONE 412·761·5666 FAX 412·261·3712

CLIFF▸KNECHT
ARTIST REPRESENTATIVE

309 WALNUT ROAD PITTSBURGH, PA 15202 PHONE 412 • 761 • 5666 FAX 412 • 261 • 3712

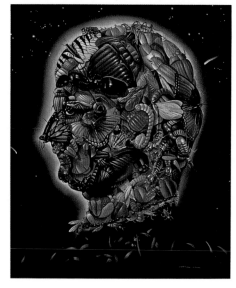

CLIFF·KNECHT
ARTIST REPRESENTATIVE

309 WALNUT ROAD PITTSBURGH, PA 15202   PHONE 412 • 761 • 5666   FAX 412 • 261 • 3712

CLIFF→KNECHT
ARTIST REPRESENTATIVE

309 WALNUT ROAD PITTSBURGH, PA 15202   PHONE 412 • 761 • 5666 FAX 412 • 261 • 3712

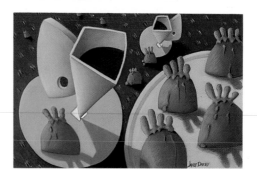

CLIFF→KNECHT
ARTIST REPRESENTATIVE

309 WALNUT ROAD PITTSBURGH, PA 15202   PHONE 412 • 761 • 5666 FAX 412 • 261 • 3712

CLIFF·KNECHT
ARTIST REPRESENTATIVE

309 WALNUT ROAD PITTSBURGH, PA 15202   PHONE 412 • 761 • 5666 FAX 412 • 261 • 3712

CLIFF→KNECHT
ARTIST REPRESENTATIVE

309 WALNUT ROAD PITTSBURGH, PA 15202   PHONE 412 • 761 • 5666 FAX 412 • 261 • 3712

CLIFF·KNECHT
ARTIST REPRESENTATIVE

309 WALNUT ROAD PITTSBURGH, PA 15202   PHONE 412 • 761 • 5666   FAX 412 • 261 • 3712

LLOYD GOLDSMITH / ILLUSTRATOR

JIM McCONNELL / ILLUSTRATOR

MAS MIYAMOTO / ILLUSTRATOR

**Square Moon
Productions**

6 MONTEREY TERRACE
ORINDA, CA 94563
Art Director:
Diane Goldsmith
(510) 253-9451   (510) 253-9452 Fax

We at SQUARE MOON are expert in matching the unique talents of illustrators to the spirit of a text. As a design studio producing books for children, we create the moment when all the elements come together to communicate the essence of a story.

SQUARE MOON represents Judith Barath, Cindy Brodie, Cheryl Harness, Ronda Hendrichsen, Pat Hoggan, Roberta Holmes-Landers, Roseanne Litzinger, Jim McConnell, Mas Miyamoto, Debbie Morse, Cindy Salans Rosenheim, Doug Roy, Carla Simmons,

Nancy Tobin, and Stan Tusan.

Clients include: Addison-Wesley, Harcourt Brace Jovanovich, Houghton Mifflin, Macmillan/McGraw Hill, McDougal Littel, Scholastic, Silver Burdett & Ginn.

CARLA SIMMONS / ILLUSTRATOR

CINDY SALANS ROSENHEIM / ILLUSTRATOR

DOUG ROY / ILLUSTRATOR

**Square Moon
Productions**

6 MONTEREY TERRACE
ORINDA, CA 94563
Art Director:
Diane Goldsmith
(510) 253-9451   (510) 253-9452 Fax

We at SQUARE MOON are expert in matching the unique talents of illustrators to the spirit of a text. As a design studio producing books for children, we create the moment when all the elements come together to communicate the essence of a story.

SQUARE MOON represents Judith Barath, Cindy Brodie, Cheryl Harness, Ronda Hendrichsen, Pat Hoggan, Roberta Holmes-Landers, Roseanne Litzinger, Jim McConnell, Mas Miyamoto, Debbie Morse, Cindy Salans Rosenheim, Doug Roy, Carla Simmons, Nancy Tobin, and Stan Tusan.

Clients include: Addison-Wesley, Harcourt Brace Jovanovich, Houghton Mifflin, Macmillan/McGraw Hill, McDougal Littel, Scholastic, Silver Burdett & Ginn.

ROSEANNE LITZINGER / ILLUSTRATOR

STAN TUSAN / ILLUSTRATOR

CINDY BRODIE / ILLUSTRATOR

RONDA HENDRICHSEN / ILLUSTRATOR

Square Moon Productions

6 Monterey Terrace
Orinda, CA 94563
Art Director:
Diane Goldsmith
(510) 253-9451   (510) 253-9452 Fax

We at SQUARE MOON are expert in matching the unique talents of illustrators to the spirit of a text. As a design studio producing books for children, we create the moment when all the elements come together to communicate the essence of a story.

SQUARE MOON represents Judith Barath, Cindy Brodie, Cheryl Harness, Ronda Hendrichsen, Pat Hoggan, Roberta Holmes-Landers, Roseanne Litzinger, Jim McConnell, Mas Miyamoto, Debbie Morse, Cindy Salans Rosenheim, Doug Roy, Carla Simmons, Nancy Tobin, and Stan Tusan.

Clients include: Addison-Wesley, Harcourt Brace Jovanovich, Houghton Mifflin, Macmillan/McGraw Hill, McDougal Littel, Scholastic, Silver Burdett & Ginn.

ROBERTA HOLMES-LANDERS / ILLUSTRATOR

NANCY TOBIN / ILLUSTRATOR

DEBBIE MORSE / ILLUSTRATOR

Square Moon Productions

6 Monterey Terrace
Orinda, CA 94563
Art Director:
Diane Goldsmith
(510) 253-9451   (510) 253-9452 Fax

We at SQUARE MOON are expert in matching the unique talents of illustrators to the spirit of a text. As a design studio producing books for children, we create the moment when all the elements come together to communicate the essence of a story.

SQUARE MOON represents Judith Barath, Cindy Brodie, Cheryl Harness, Ronda Hendrichsen, Pat Hoggan, Roberta Holmes-Landers, Roseanne Litzinger, Jim McConnell, Mas Miyamoto, Debbie Morse, Cindy Salans Rosenheim, Doug Roy, Carla Simmons, Nancy Tobin, and Stan Tusan.

Clients include: Addison-Wesley, Harcourt Brace Jovanovich, Houghton Mifflin, Macmillan/McGraw Hill, McDougal Littel, Scholastic, Silver Burdett & Ginn.

PG | REPRESENTATIVES
VISUAL COMMUNICATION

PAT HEROUX GOUDREAU

4 TIF 1 3   9 E6A 7   9 8 L5 5
4 1 3   9 6 7   3 2 X9 3

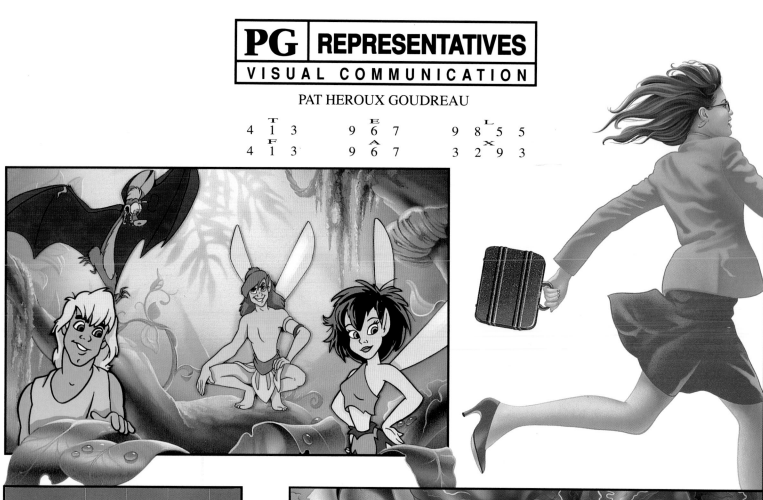

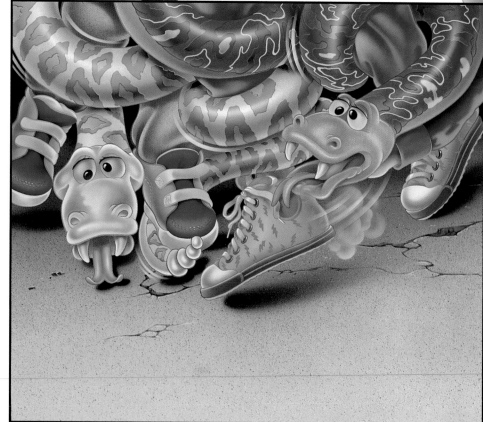

Roc Goudreau

P.G. REPRESENTATIVES
STONEMILL MARKET PLACE
EAST MAIN STREET, P.O. BOX 322
WARE, MA 01082
(413) 967-9855
FAX (413) 967-3293

Clients include:
Milton Bradley
Columbia Pictures
Twentieth Century Fox
Disney
Hasbro
E.R.O. Industries

Smith & Wesson
International Games
Western Publishing
BF Goodrich
T.S.R. Inc.
Spalding
Mirage

Totsy
S.L.M., Inc.
Kenner
Mattel
Sesame Street

PG | REPRESENTATIVES
VISUAL COMMUNICATION
PAT HEROUX GOUDREAU

T				E				L		
4	1	3	9	6	7	9	8	5	5
T F				E A				X		
4	1	3	9	6	7	3	2	9	3

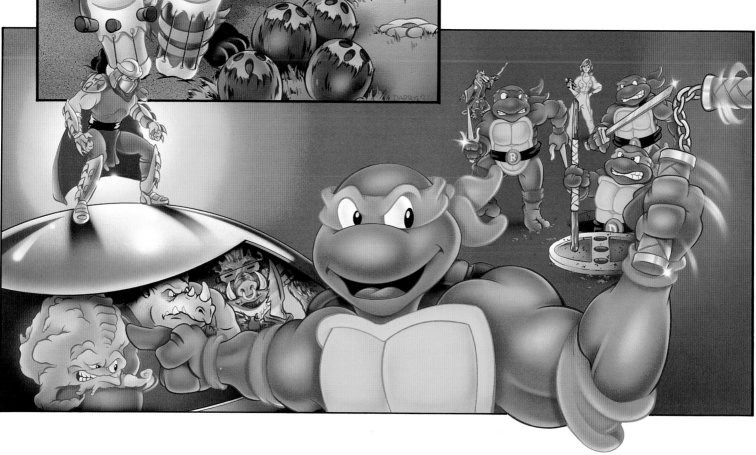

Darryl Goudreau

P.G. Representatives
Stonemill Market Place
East Main Street, P.O. Box 322
Ware, MA 01082
(413) 967-9855
Fax (413) 967-3293

Clients include:
Milton Bradley
Columbia Pictures
Twentieth Century Fox
Disney
Hasbro
E.R.O. Industries

Smith & Wesson
International Games
Western Publishing
BF Goodrich
T.S.R. Inc.
Spalding
Mirage

Totsy
S.L.M., Inc.
Kenner
Mattel
Sesame Street

PAT HEROUX GOUDREAU

4 T 3   9 E 7   9 8 L 5 5
  1   6   5
4 F 3   9 A 7   3 2 X 9 3
  1   6

Jonathan Weisbach

P.G. Representatives
Stonemill Market Place
East Main Street, P.O. Box 322
Ware, MA 01082

(413) 967-9855   (413) 967-3293

Clients include:
Milton Bradley
Columbia Pictures
Twentieth Century Fox
Disney
Hasbro
E.R.O. Industries

Smith & Wesson
International Games
Western Publishing
BF Goodrich
T.S.R. Inc.
Spalding
Mirage

Totsy
S.L.M., Inc.
Kenner
Mattel
Sesame Street

Rodino R. Bautista

ROD • WATER • DESIGN
1193 BAYARD DRIVE
SAN JOSE, CALIFORNIA 95122

PHONE & FAX (408) 297-0325

Clients:
Emperor Production
World Premiere affiliated with
Universal Studios
Medical publishing
Advertising agencies
I.P.T. Corporation

Novel artist
Different variety of magazines
Advertised for food corporations
Editorial
Electronic illustration
Medical
Portraits

Product
Science Fiction
Story Boards
Technical

JOHN S. DYKES

17 Morningside Dr. S. ☐ Westport, CT 06880 ☐ (203) 222-8150 Fax 222-8155

Client: Medical Economics

Client: Harvard Business School

Client: Harvard Business School

MICHELE
NOISET
617-542-2731
FAX-422-0298

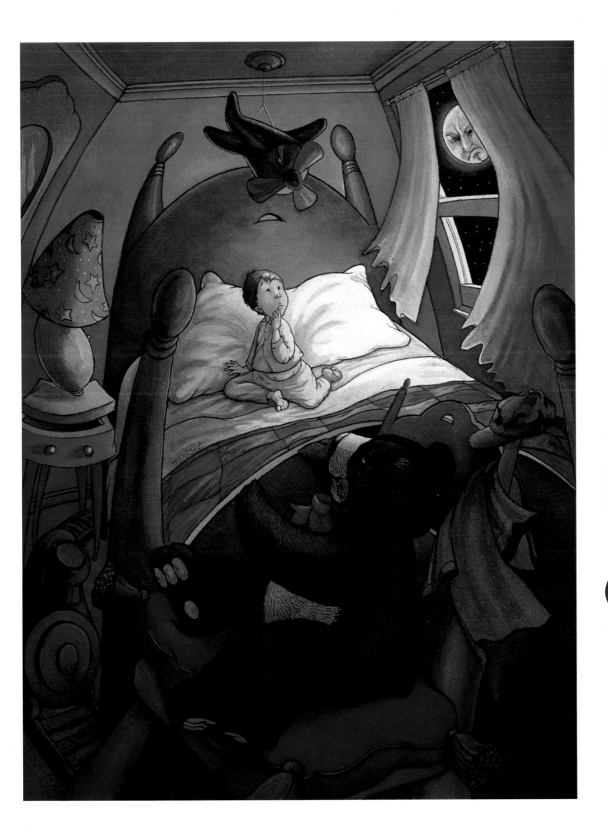

MIDWEST REPRESENTATION
KORALIK ASSOCIATES
312-944-5680
FAX-421-5948

Douglas R. Chezem   703·591·5424
Fax·591·4825

Separations of Digital Art by Executive Presentations, Inc., Rockville, Maryland.

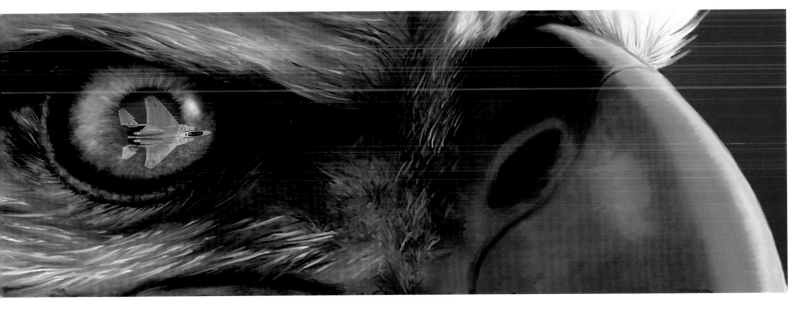

Douglas R. Chezem 703·591·5424
Fax·591·4825

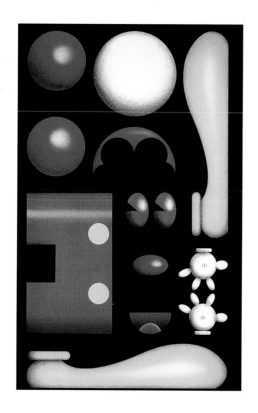

164 daniel low terrace si ny 10301   (718) 727 0723   fax (718) 727 0927

Terry
Allen

164 daniel low terrace si ny 10301   (718) 727 0723   fax (718) 727 0927

Terry

Allen

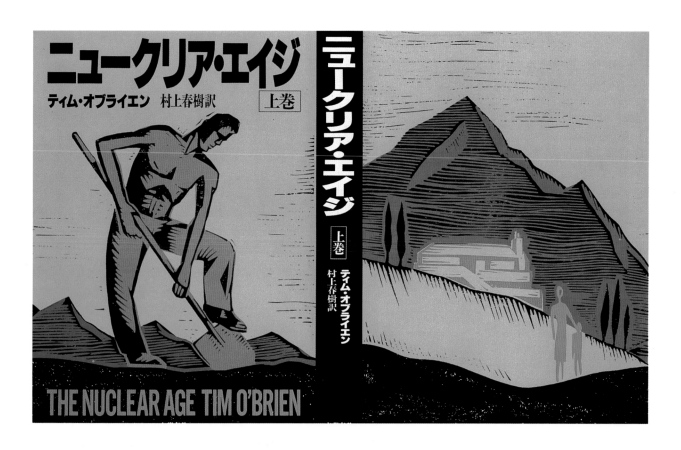

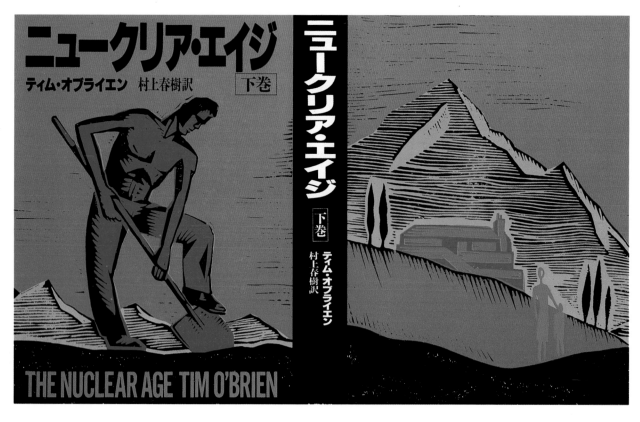

Renee
Klein

164 daniel low terrace si ny 10301   (212) 522 4464   or   (718) 727 0723

164 daniel low terrace si ny 10301   (212) 522 4464   or   (718) 727 0723

Ken Fallin

25 Windsor Road
Milton, MA 02186

(617) 696-2677
(212) 362-7646

Clients include:
American Express
Boston Magazine
"Forbidden Broadway"
Ladies Home Journal
Ogilvy & Mather
"Crazy For You"

The Boston Herald
Showtime
Atlanta Magazine
Harvard University
The Detroit Free Press
The Hartford Courant
Mark Taper Forum

Member Graphic Artists Guild

PAUL HAMILL
ILLUSTRATION
408 · 280 · 0879
1009 EMPEY WAY   SAN JOSE, CA. 95128

© Simon & Schuster

© Simon & Schuster

Zita Asbaghi

104-40 Queens Blvd. Apt. #12X
Forest Hills, New York 11375

(718) 275-1995

ZITA ASBAGHI

(718) 275-1995

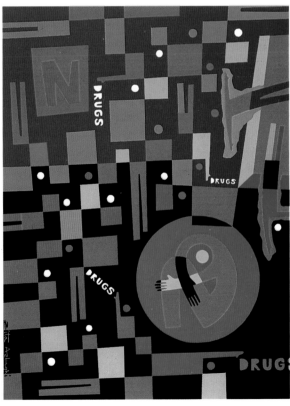

phone
818
301
9662

fax
818
303
1123

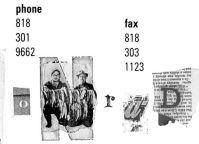

jon conrad

221 west maple street monrovia california 91016

BUDWEISER - national ads

AMERICAN WAY MAGAZINES - triathaletes

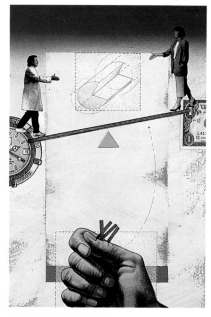

BAXTER PHARMACEUTICAL - capabilities

SPORTS ILLUSTRATED FOR KIDS - olympic spirit

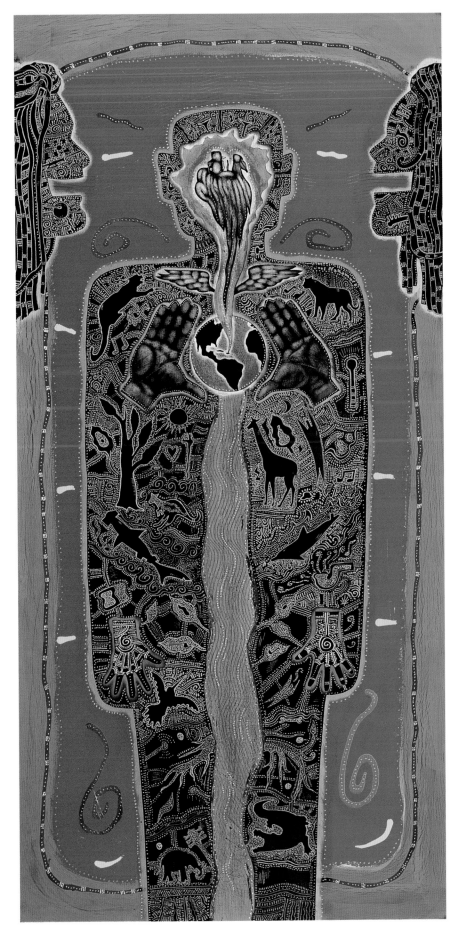

WAILING SOULS / SONY MUSIC

BALTIMORE SYMPHONY

GILBERT PAPER

Joel Nakamura Paintings · Illustrations · 818·301·0177 · Fax 818·303·1123

Kelly Akins

29023 Rolando Road
Lake Elsinore, CA 92530

(909) 674-6124

Clients include:

NFL, NBA, many Major League Baseball teams, 20th Century Fox, Universal Pictures, Concorde Pictures, Shell Oil, Kelloggs, Hughes Aircraft, Educational Insights, Maiden Sunshine Beach Towels, Chevrolet, Chart House

Restaurants, Carnation, and many fine art investors.

"GOOD·GIRL" GRAPHICS

JERRY ACERNO
3455 JASMINE AVENUE, #19
LOS ANGELES, CA 90034
310-842-9728

ILLUSTRATION · CARTOONING · STORYBOARDS

Nishan Akgulian

42-29 64TH STREET

WOODSIDE, NY 11377

PHONE & FAX (718) 565-6936

Bugle Boy

Coors Brewing Co.

SCOTT angle

21051
Barbados
Circle
Huntington
Beach, CA
92646

714
960
8485

Mr. totally Bitchin' Sun-Worshiper and Love God...

TRISH · BURGIO

8205 SANTA MONICA BLVD · STE 1-244 · LOS ANGELES, CA. 90046 · (310) 657-1469

TRISH · BURGIO

8205 SANTA MONICA BLVD. · STE. 1-244 · LOS ANGELES, CA. 90046 · (310) 657-1469

David Scott Meier

P.O. Box 353
Laguna Beach, CA 92652-0353

(714) 494-4206

I find you fascinating; is it your cologne or your budget? No air-brushed cola cans here. Instead, I offer you lots of pattern and quick turn-around time. You'd paint this way, too, if you hung out at the Getty and wore thick glasses.

Sure, I'm published; call for information.

Alfred Ramage

SILENT SOUNDS STUDIO
5 IRWIN STREET
WINTHROP, MA 02152

(617) 846-5955
FAX IN STUDIO

Member Graphic Artists Guild

Also see: *Graphic Artists Guild's Directory of Illustration 5, 6, 7, 8.*

"User friendly"

Media: Oil, ink, watercolor, collage, colored pencil, mixed.

Expertise: Editorial, book cover, advertising, 3D action premiums, graphics, exhibit design.

©Alfred Ramage 1992

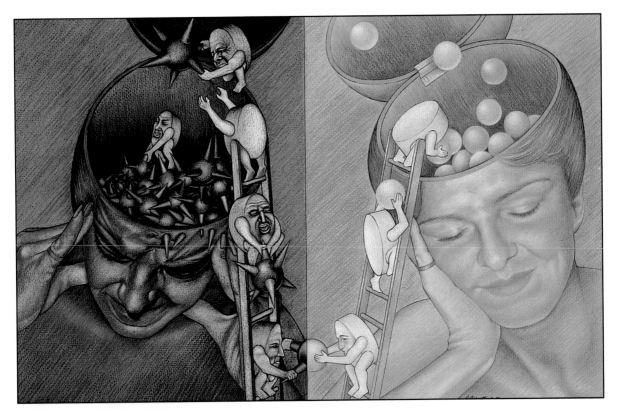

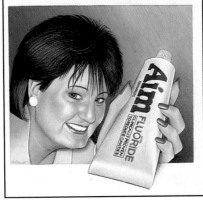

Debby Barrett
49 HAMILTON STREET
EVERETT, MA 02149

(617) 387-2031

Client list:
Cahners Publishing, *EDN Magazine,*
Modern Materials Handling, Elec-
tronics Purchasing, Paper Magic,
Sundance Publishing, Silver Burdett
& Ginn, Meadow Glen Mall, Polaroid,
Raytheon, MIT, Sandoz Pharmaceuti-
cals, Armatron International, Boston
Federal Savings Bank, Woburn Five.

Graphic Artists Guild Member

Larry Ross
53 FAIRVIEW AVENUE
MADISON, NJ 07940

(201) 377-6859
FAX AVAILABLE IN STUDIO

My clients include: (satisfied and delighted) National, Regional, and Local Ad Agencies, Magazines, Children's Book Publishers, and Design Studios.

An animation reel is available.

For additional work: American Showcase 13 and RSVP 17.

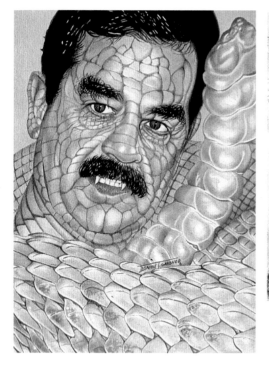

Bonnie T. Gardner

142 W. 19TH STREET
NEW YORK, NY 10011

(212) 255-0863

Clients include: Ciba Geigy, FLM
Graphics, Gallery Magazine, Oui Maga-
zine, Doubleday Publishing, M. Evans
& Co. Inc., American Express, United
Way, All Star Communications, Epic
Security, Evergreen Press, Interconti-
nental Greeting Card Co., Marian

Heath Greetings, Office Life, IMS
America, National Review Magazine,
Downtown Express, Futurific Magazine, and various private portrait
commissions.

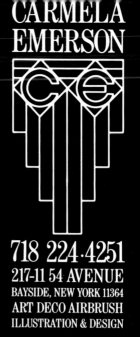

CARMELA
EMERSON

718 224·4251

217-11 54 AVENUE

BAYSIDE, NEW YORK 11364

ART DECO AIRBRUSH

ILLUSTRATION & DESIGN

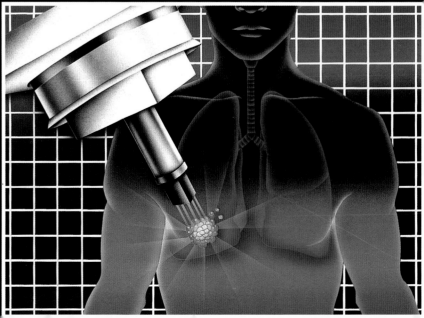

JIM CARSON

1-2-3 Under
OPEN LOOK
Clicks
With Sun.

See what Lotus® has
just done for Sun®
SPARC® System
users.

BLUE CROSS BLUE SHIELD
ALL KINDS OF PEOPLE.
ALL KINDS OF PLANS.

All through
October,

All through
November,

And all through
December.

(617) 661-3321

11 FOCH ST. CAMBRIDGE, MA 02140

LOTZA CLIENTS, AWARDS, EXPERIENCE

Peter Bianco

ILLUSTRATOR

BiancoMarchilonisDesign

348 Manning Street

Needham, MA 02192

Tel/Fax (617) 444-9077

Whimsical and humorous illustrations for corporate communications, direct mail, advertising and publishing.
To view additional work, please see the Graphic Artists Guild Directory #8.

Member Graphic Artists Guild

© 1992, 1993 Peter Bianco

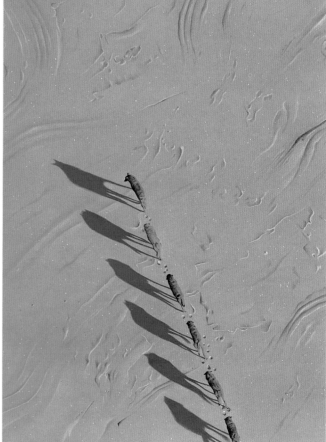

Sal Catalano

114 BOYCE PLACE
RIDGEWOOD, NJ 07450

(201) 447-5318

Clients include:
National Audubon Society, Ciba Geigy, Hoffman La Roche, CBS, NBC, Coca-Cola, General Foods, N.Y. Zoological Society, Canada Dry, ABC, Time/Life, Pepsi-Cola, Citibank, Travenol, U.S. Government, Upjohn, Lederle, Pfizer, Winthrop, Burger King, IBM, DuPont, United Artists, Sony, Panasonic, Borden, McGraw/Hill, RCA, TWA, McNeil, Squibb, Wyeth, Sterling, American Distillers, N.J. Bell, Paramount Studios, Merck, The Rockefeller Group, Paine Webber, Avon Books, HarperCollins, National Wildlife Federation, *Reader's Digest,* American Museum of Natural History, Exxon, Becton Dickinson, *Field & Stream, TV Guide, Smithsonian, The New Yorker, N.Y. Times.*

Susan Greenstein
4915 SURF AVENUE
BROOKLYN, NEW YORK 11224

PHONE & FAX (718) 373-4475

New Woman Magazine, Audio Magazine, John Wiley & Sons Publishing, Cornell University, Travel & Leisure Magazine, American Booksellers Association, The New York Times, Len Dugow & Associates, Business Tokyo Magazine, Pentagram Design, Global Finance Magazine, Walker & Co. Publishing, Brooklyn AIDS Task Force, Muscular Dystrophy Association, Applause Magazine, Deutsch Design, IBM, Modern Maturity Magazine, Restaurant Business Magazine, Scholastic Publishing, Continental Insurance, Changing Times Magazine, McGraw-Hill, Inc., Ronn Campisi Design, Lotus, The Brooklyn Children's Museum, Harcourt Brace Jovanovich Inc., Carbone Smolan Design, MacMillan Publishing, The Daily News

Patrick O. Chapin
Illustrator

Portfolio available upon request.
(216) 234-6890

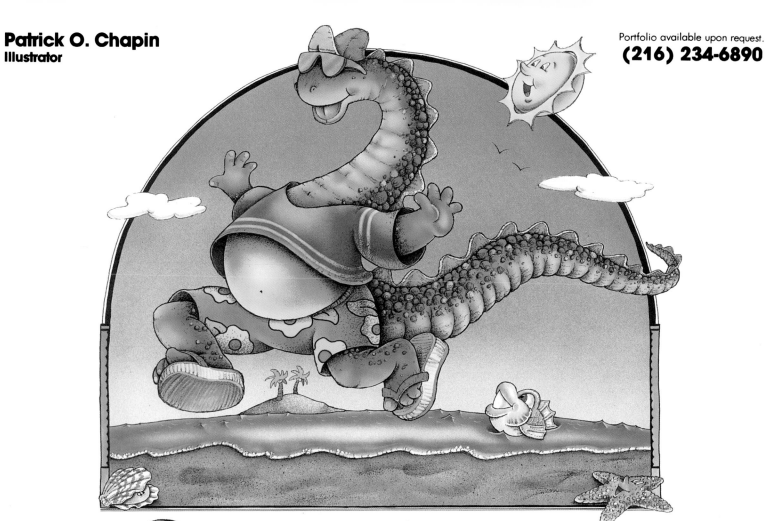

177 W. Bridge Dr. • **Berea OH 44017** • **Fax (216) 234-6890**✻

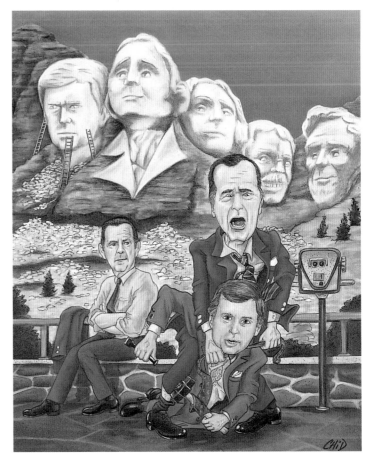

CHiD

55 Desmond Avenue
Bronxville, NY 10708

Phone/Fax (914) 793-5220

THE NEXT TIME YOU THINK
VISUAL . . .
THINK CHiD.
STYLIZED ILLUSTRATION FOR ALL
APPLICATIONS.

Portfolio and list of clientele available
upon request.
Work also appears in the Graphic
Artists Guild Directory of Illustration:
Volumes 6, 7, 8.
The Creative Source Book: 6th edition
Member Graphic Artists Guild

SMART ART
HIGH CONCEPT HUMOR

Southern Fried Pizza Eatin' Chicken
Sports Illustrated For Kids

Youngest Depositers Get P.C. Link
Bank Systems and Technology

The 1991 Emmy Awards   *N.Y. Newsday T.V. Plus*

M.e. COHeN
212 627 8033

M.E. Cohen
95 Horatio Street 10M
New York, NY 10014

(212) 627-8033

Clients include: Newsweek, Time-Warner, New York Times, Ogilvy & Mather, Pizza Hut, Arthur D. Little, Sesame Street, Wall Street Journal, U.S. News & World Report, USA Today, Business Week, Barrons, Newsday, E.O.S. Corporation, D.D.B. Needham, Ziff-Davis, American Management Association, Hearst, Boston Globe, Press-Enterprise, et. al.

Art Glazer
2 JAMES ROAD
MT. KISCO, NY 10549

(914) 666-4554

DAVE

Clegg

multi-purpose illustration

(404) 887·6306
fax 781·5780

Maybe You've Outgrown Your Checking Account, Too.

Ask about GuarantyPak℠ or Guaranty Gold.℠

Rep'd by → Susan Wells & Associates   (404) 255·1430   fax 255·3449

TREEEE TUUUU WANNN

end

DAVE

Clegg

multi-purpose illustration

(404) 887·6306
fax 781·5780

Rep'd by

Susan Wells & Associates

(404) 255·1430
fax 255·3449

I'd commit this information to memory.

yup.

HARD-NOSED SALES, INK.

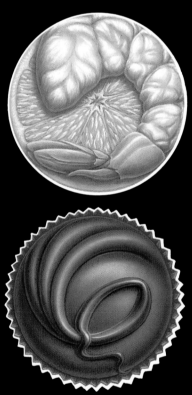

Sue Ellen Brown

4212 Delmar Avenue
Dallas, Texas 75206
(214) 823-9545
Fax available

LESLIE MONTANA
35 LEXINGTON AVE.
MONTCLAIR N.J.
07042
·
VOICE: 201.744-3407
FAX: 201.746-4636

Andrea Baruffi

341 Hudson Terrace
Piermont, NY 10968

Phone and Fax (914) 359-9542

Did you hear the one about
the Marketing Director who missed
the $20 billion golf market?

Andrea Baruffi

341 Hudson Terrace
Piermont, NY 10968

Phone and Fax (914) 359-9542

Catherine Jones

P.O. Box 6309
Santa Fe, NM 87502

(505) 986-8629
Fax in studio

Jean Hirashima
166 E. 61ST STREET 5 C
NEW YORK, NY 10021

(212) 593-9778

J.D. King

158 Sixth Av.,
Bklyn, NY 11217
(718) 636-0768
Fax: (718) 399-6427

CLIENT LIST:

Adweek
Anthony Russell Inc.
The Boston Globe
Business Week
Comedy Central
The Detroit Free Press
Fortune
Frankfurt Gipps Balkind
Grand Marnier Liqueur
J.J. Sedelmaier Prod.
Manufacturers Hanover
MasterCard
The N.Y. Daily News
Nick at Nite
The Progressive
Sony
Sub Pop Records
Time Warner
Town & Country
The Utne Reader
The Village Voice
The Wall St. Journal
The Washington Post
Whittle Communications

AWARDS:

American Illustration 9
C.A. Annual '92
AIGA Graphic Design USA: 14

Entertainment Weekly

New York Magazine

ABSOLUT KING.

Absolut Vodka

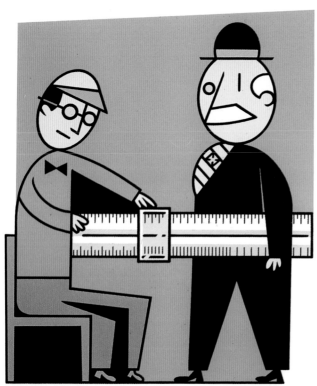

The Art of Mickey Mouse/ © The Walt Disney Co.

John F. Dyess

JOHN DYESS ILLUSTRATION
703 JOSEPHINE AVENUE
GLENDALE, MO 63122

PHONE & FAX (314) 822-2893

I have been a commercial illustrator since graduating from Washington University, St. Louis in 1961. I have appeared in the following: Sports Afield, Field and Stream, Highlights for Children, Popular Mechanics, T.V. Guide. Some of the Clients I have worked for during the last three years include: Anheuser-Busch, Cigna Corporation, Continental Baking, Harcourt Brace Jovanovich, Silver Burdett Co., Southwestern Bell, Pet Inc., Boyds Mill Press, Ducks Unlimited.

Paulette Bogan
(212) 243-1694

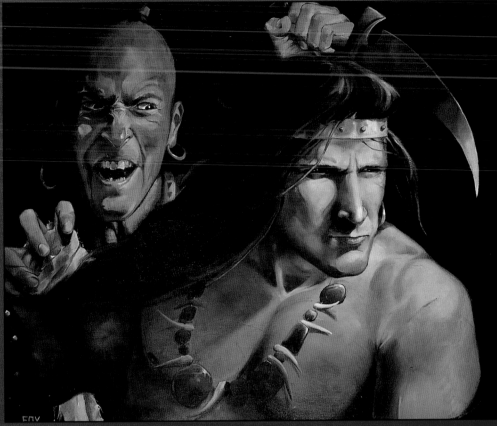

Brian T. Fox

Fantasy Illustration

29 Massasoit Street
Somerset, Massachusetts 02725

(508) 674-0511

ALAN NAHIGIAN

33-08 31st Avenue #2R, Long Island City, NY 11106-1440   (718) 274-4042

DEAN FLEMING

818·795·4636

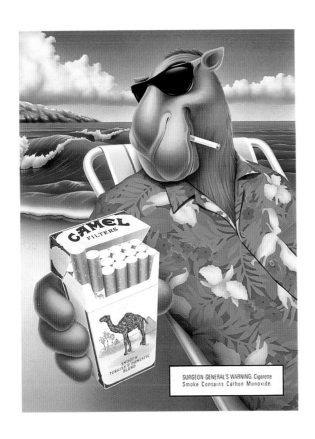

John T. Ward

20 BIRCH STREET
SARANAC LAKE, NY 12983

PHONE   (518) 891-4534
FAX   (518) 891-4534

Campbell Laird

212·5055552

©1992 Nancy Lee Walter

©1992 World Book Publishing

©1992 Nancy Lee Walter

Nancy Lee Walter

391 POPLAR AVENUE
ELMHURST, ILLINOIS 60126-4011

(708) 833-3898
FAX (708) 833-6685

Children's and editorial subjects, science, animals. Gouache, ink, graphite, colored pencil, and combinations. Art for print, film and video. Samples are available, upon request.

Accounts: Lincoln Park Zoo • Motorola Museum of Electronics • General Exhibits & Displays • World Book Publishing • Childcraft • Encyclopedia Britannica/Compton's • Scott, Foresman and Company • Ligature, Inc. • Nystrom • The Quarasan Group, Inc. •

Publicom, Inc. • David C. Cook Publishing Company • Mlodock Hansen • Studio 111 • Vogele Stoic Associates, Inc. • Garfield Linn & Company • Wells, Rich, Green, Inc. • Coronet/MTI Film & Video

SMOKING

C Magazine

Why I Quit Working at Paolo's

CHERYL FUSCO

Some people look easily into mirrors. Clara, the woman who cuts my hair, for example, stops snipping sometimes to smile at her own broad face in the beauty-shop mirror. Even with me watching, she can adjust her collar or tug her smock down over her bottom and look at herself. Clara's not young, she was certainly never a beauty, but she knows something important that I'm trying hard to learn.

When she finishes my haircut, Clara always gives me a hand mirror. "How do you like it?" she asks.

I used to say, "It's fine, Clara. Thanks." But I wouldn't really look in Clara's mirrors. It was too hard for me to do that.

Time has helped some. I'm almost twenty now, and my face doesn't look like it did. Slight scars are there, though. Both inside and out. A doe tilting its head toward the glare of my headlights is all I can remember about that day. Yet my hands still shake every time I grasp the steering wheel of a car. It doesn't matter, though. I can't afford to buy my own car yet. By the time I can, things may be different. Meanwhile, I ride my bike in good weather and take the bus when it's bad.

n't look in Clara's mirrors or in anyone
Paolo's Pizza and Sandwich Shoppe,
ht. I remember everything about that
de my bike to work:
s I coast down Pine Street, are the low
at the mirror covering the upper half
e more.
stop for traffic and focus on things I
ple order at the counter and eat there
nt to sit. I don't prepare food. Upstairs
whole-wheat crust and constructs
alfalfa sprouts, tofu, and raisins.

DAVE ROSS

DAVE ROSS

ILLUSTRATION
531 41ST STREET
BROOKLYN NY 11232
7 1 8 • 8 5 4 • 1 0 0 6

merican Bar Examiner Magazine

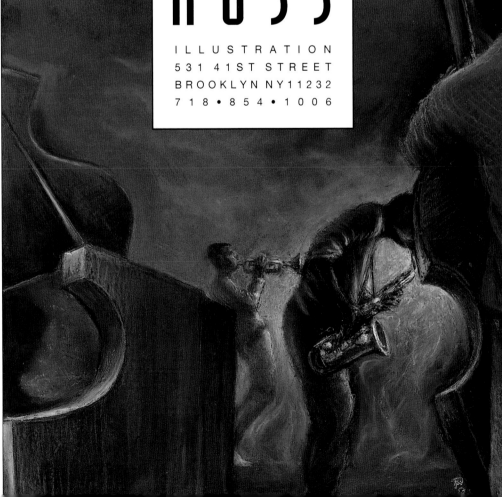

Nikki Middendorf

200 East 28 Street #2-B
New York, NY 10016

(212) 683-2848

Clockwise from left:
1. Business Week
2. Wall Street Journal
3. New York Times

Redbook

Men's Health

Sport's Illustrated

Entertainment Weekly

Robert Valentine Inc:
Fashion Follies

DAVID SHELDON

PHONE & FAX: (606) 261-4947 • ANIMATION REEL AVAILABLE ON REQUEST

Bill Fricke

GRAFFIC JAM

426 ADAMSTON ROAD

BRICK, NJ 08723

(908) 477-5482

Fax (908) 920-3793

GRAFFIC CLIENTS:

CMP Publications

New York Times Book Review

CitiBank, NY

G.P. Putnam and Sons

Art Directors' Club of N.J.

N.J. Audubon Society

GRAFFIC ROAD TRIP!

Get all your mental baggage.

Let's make tracks.

Comfy? O.K., if we both drive.

You see, this vehicle runs on

concepts. My tank is ALWAYS

FULL. Even if yours isn't!

Let's take the Scenic Route.

We'll experience images at

the *Speed of Sight* that'll

BLOW YOUR DOORS IN!

Remember, you're not really

movin' till you're in a

GRAFFIC JAM.

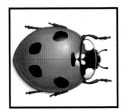

Theodor Lloyd Glazer

WESTVIEW STUDIO
28 WESTVIEW ROAD
SPRING VALLEY, NY 10977

TEL: (914) 354-1524
FAX: (914) 354-1682

Clients include: AAA, Avon, Dannon, Dial, EM Industries, GRP Records, The Gannett Group, Hayden Publishing, MCA Records, Nestlé Foods, Philips Records, Quality Exports of Indonesia, Rockland Center for the Arts, Sterling Winthrop International, Viking/Penguin, Warner Home Video Inc.

. . . a creative resource for illustration design solutions.

2 1 2 · 8 6 1 · 7 1 7 8

j o d y · w h e e l e r

509 east 78th st. · 6e · n.y. n.y. · 10021

clients: Gordon Fraser   Ideals   Simon & Schuster   Warner Books
           Grosset & Dunlop   Random House   Viking Penguin   Western Publishing

Sophia Latto

723 PRESIDENT STREET
BROOKLYN, NY 11215

(718) 789-1980

Client List:
American Banker
American Express
American Management Association
Doubleday
Cardiology News
Cooper-Hewitt Museum

Hudson River Museum
Laguna Sportswear
Lynch, Jones & Ryan
Macmillan/McGraw-Hill
Medical Communique
New York City Transit Authority
Oxford University Press

Pennsylvania Hospital
Resortworks
Smithsonian Magazine
The Salvation Army

Member: Graphic Artists Guild and
Society of Illustrators

LINDA SCHIWALL

10 HIGHLAND AVENUE
NORTHAMPTON
MASSACHUSETTS 01060
413 ~ 584 ~ 5094

ANTHONY MARTIN
Illustration
▼

212·677·1060

Winson Trang
2233 W. Main Street #K
Alhambra, CA 91801

(818) 570-8718
Fax (818) 308-3464

Member of the San Francisco Society
of Illustrators

148

Leyla Torres

718.389.6101 • 14 North Henry Street, Brooklyn NY 11222

Suzette Barbier

inchester St., Newton, MA 02161   Phone 617/527·8388 ■ Fax 617/244·0266

STUDIOS

Julia Talcott

38 Linden St., Brookline, MA 02146 Phone 617/232·7306 ■ Fax in Studio

68 Agassiz Ave., Belmont, MA 02178   Phone 617/484·8023 ▪ Fax Available

27 Wyman St., Arlington, MA 02174   Phone 617/646·0785 ■ Fax Ava

DON MORRISON

FANNY MELLET BERRY

ADAM SMITH

HAL JUST

JERRY MCDANIEL

ILLUSTRATION & COMPUTER ART

Anita Grien
155 East 38th Street
New York, NY 10016

(212) 697-6170
Fax (212) 697-6177

Representing:
Fanny Mellet Berry
Don Morrison
Hal Just
Jerry McDaniel

Pat Porter

28 West 69th Street
New York, N.Y. 10023

212 799-8493

ABCDEFG

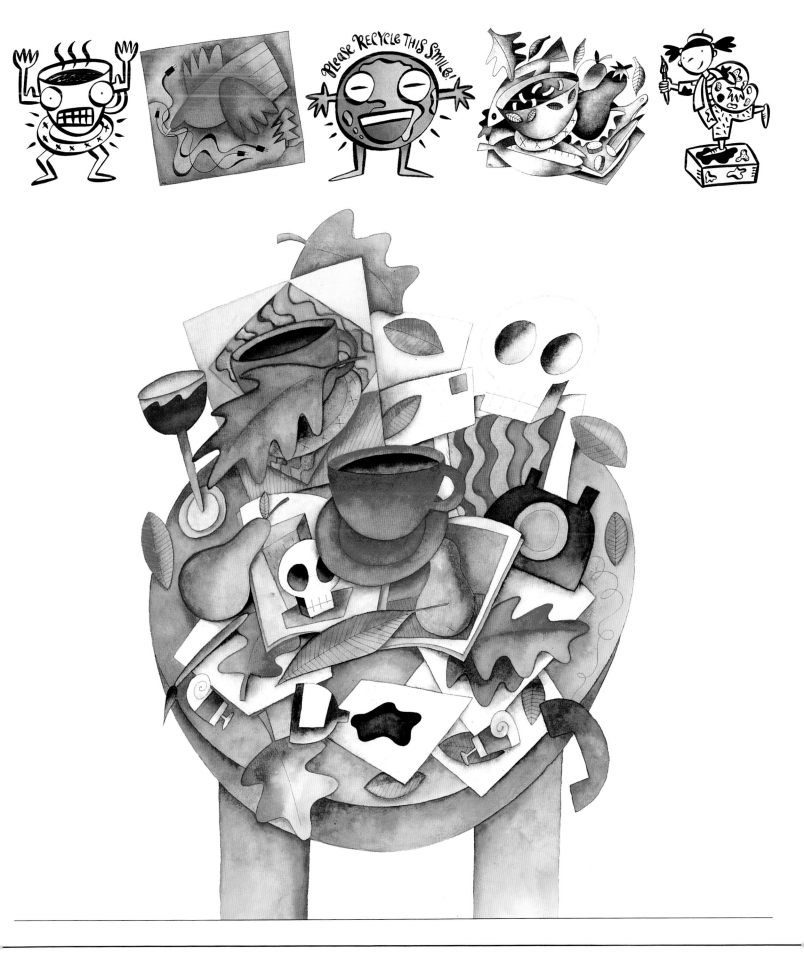

Mary Anne Lloyd

Represented by:
Sharon Kurlansky
192 Southville Road
Southboro, Massachusetts 01772
Phone: (508) 872-4549
Fax: (508) 460-6058

Clients include:
Atlantic Monthly, Boston Globe,
Boston Pops, Bostonia Magazine, CIO
Magazine, Corey McPherson Nash, East
West Journal, Horticulture Magazine,
MacMillan/McGraw Hill, MIT Technology Review, New Age Journal, New
England Business Magazine, New York
Times, Nickelodeon Cable Television,
Playboy, Ronn Campisi Design, Scholastic Magazine, TNT Cable Network,
Vestron Motion Pictures, Whittle
Communications.

Joel F. Naprstek
76 Park Place
Morris Plains, NJ 07950

(201) 285-0692

- Freelance illustrator since 1972
- Taught illustration 8 years SVA, presently at Joe Kubert School
- Acrylic on flexible surface
- B&W also, paint, pencil
- Editorial, advertising, books, young readers, automotive, aviation, medical, corporate, humor
- Portraits and mural work
- Draw and paint all types of subject matter
- Easy to work with
- Never miss deadlines

Clients: AT&T, Consumer Electronics, Tundra Pub., Children's Television Workshop, Steve Phillips Design, Scholastic, NBC, CBS, Fortune, Business Week, Cablevision, Bell Labs, Raintree Pub., Random House, McGraw-Hill, Time Inc., American Tobacco Co.

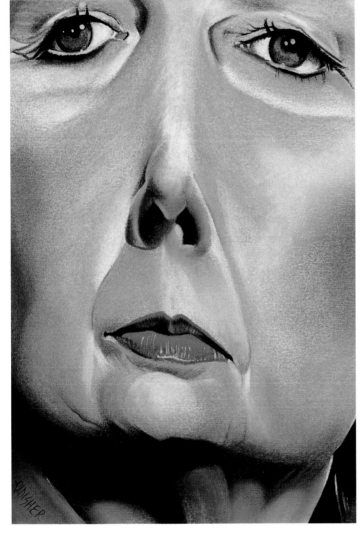

Martha Gradisher

245 PIERMONT AVENUE
SOUTH NYACK, NY 10960

PHONE & FAX (914) 358-0185

Clients include: ABC News; NBC Radio
Entertainment; PC Magazine; Wells
Fargo Bank International; Chembank
(Manufacturer's Hanover); Gannett
Suburban Newspapers; Harriet Ziefert,
Inc.; Big Baby Co.; Business Week.

Member:
Society of Children's Book Writers
Graphic Artists Guild

DONNA SCHILLER
Advertising · Editorial · Book
914·897·2218

Humorous Illustration
Caricature

THE SUICIDE COOKBOOK

MOODY
212·989·8017

Judith Arlene Pate
699 County Home Road
Reidsville, NC 27320

(919) 342 DRAW

Member Graphic Artists Guild

Hidden Pictures
Anthropomorphization
Children's Art
Line Drawing

©Judith Arlene Pate

BILL·ERSLAND

BOX 556 · STILLWATER, MN 55082 · (612) 430 · 1878

JACQUI MORGAN

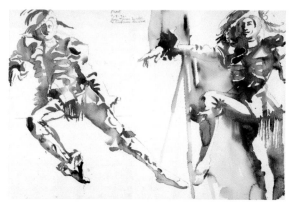

NUVEEN

Enjoy Life's Sweet Rewards

Ask Us About Steady, Tax-Free Income from Nuveen

Fidelity Investments®

Clients include: American Express, Architectural Digest, AT&T, CPC Int'l., Champion Papers, Citibank, Colgate Palmolive, Corporate Annual Reports,, Corporate Graphics, Inc., Eli Lilly, Esquire Magazine, Family Circle, First National Supermarkets, General Foods, Hilton Int'l, IBM, INC Design, ITC,, ITT Sheraton, Kellogg's, Kinney Shoes, Kmart, Kraft, Lear's, Merck Pharmaceutical, New Woman, New York Hospital for Special Surgery, New York Magazine, New York Times, Nuveen, Outdoor Life, Oxford University Press, Proctor & Gamble, Rodale Press, St. Francis College, Scott Paper Co., Seiko, Self Magazine, South Bell, Stolichnaya, TIAA-CREF, Wechsler & Partners, Woman's Day, Ziff-Davis.

JACQUI MORGAN STUDIO • 692 GREENWICH STREET • NEW YORK, NY 10014 • 212 • 463 • 8488 • FAX • 463 • 8688

Jack A. Lutzow

JAL ASSOCIATES, INC.
12305 MANZANITA LANE
GLEN ELLEN, CA 95442

(415) 929-1369   Fax (415) 292-7050

Comprehensive illustration that will make your creative ideas desirable. My renderings of foods and non-foods have been used for such firms as Carnation, Del Monte, Dole, Green Giant, Hills Bros., Hunt, Kroger, Pillsbury, Post, Quaker Oats, Ralston Purina, and Safeway.

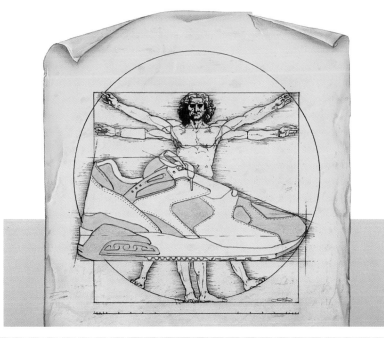

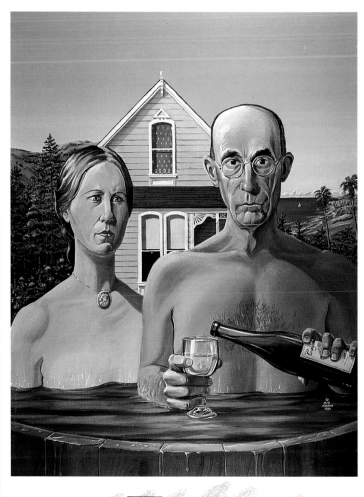

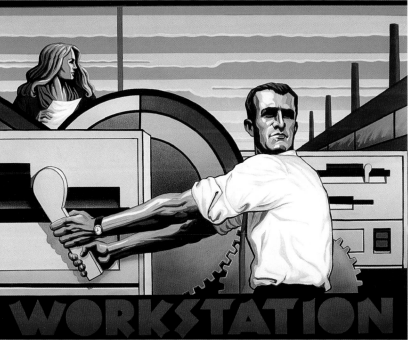

J·T· MORROW
THE ART OF IMITATION
(415) 355-7899   Fax in Studio

© 1992, J.T. Morrow

From Stone Age to contemporary art, I'll give you the look you're looking for!

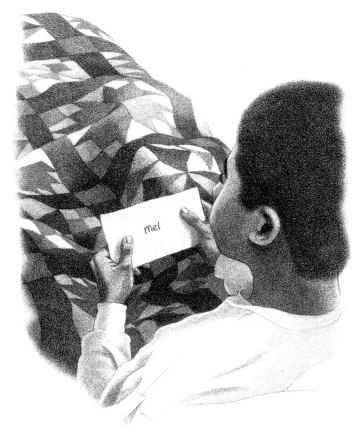

Karen Meyer

P.O. Box 191

Saratoga Springs, NY 12866

(518) 581-0310

Finely rendered, light filled pencil drawings for editorial, advertising and children's books.

Additional illustrations may be seen in Directory of Illustration #8, under the name Karen Meyer Swearingen.

JAMES MELLETT (412) 563-4131

Suzanne Shimek Dunaway

10211 CHRYSANTHEMUM LANE
LOS ANGELES, CALIFORNIA 90077

TEL: (310) 470-1914
FAX: (310) 470-2050

A sampling of clients:
The New Yorker, Gourmet Magazine, The Los Angeles Times (Food, Travel and Book Review), Gault/Millau America, Loew's Hotels, Avery Restaurant Supply, The Grill, Il Forno Los Angeles, Il Forno Rapongo, The Ritz Carlton, Wolfgang Puck, *L.A. West, The Arkansas Times,* The American Institute of Wine & Food, The Bombay Cafe, The Authentic Cafe, and others.

Valerie Costantino

2037 New Hyde Park Road
New Hyde Park, NY 11040

(516) 358-9121

©Valerie Costantino

Vicki Wehrman

(716) 657-7910 • FAX: (716) 657-7545 • BOX 146 • E. BLOOMFIELD • NEW YORK • 14443

dickran PALULIAN

REPRESENTATIVE: JOANNE PALULIAN
212·581·8338
203·866·3734
FAX#203·857·0842

Andrew Shiff

153 Clinton Street
Hopkinton, MA 01748

(508) 435-3607
Fax (508) 435-5625

Clients include: D.C. Heath, Digital, EMS, Ground Round, Hanover Insurance, Harcourt Brace Jovanovich, Houghton Mifflin, John Hancock, Jordan Marsh, Macmillan, Marriott, McDonald's, Oxford University Press, Raytheon, Sheraton, Silver Burdett & Ginn, State Mutual Companies, Sugarloaf Inn Resort, Texas Instruments.

Member: Graphic Artists Guild

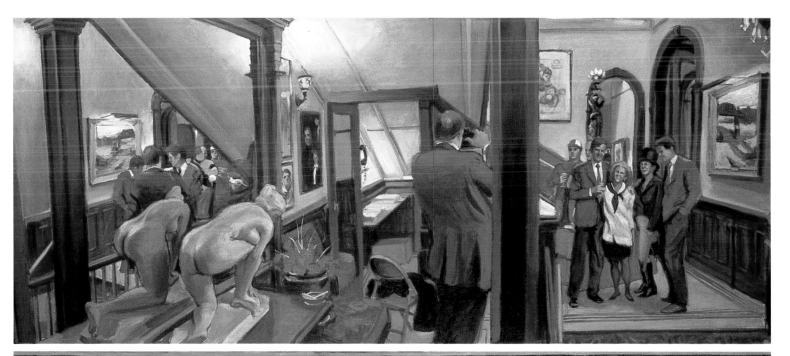

Thomas Thorspecken

615 East 14 Street #7A
New York, NY 10009

(212) 995-5647

Clients include:

Harper & Row
Paragon House
Business Week
Scholastic Publications
American Kennel Club
Consumer Electronics

Corporate Finance
Fame
The Scientist
Home Office Computing
The Daily News
The American Journal of Nursing
Holt Reinhart & Winston

SIGS Publications
Circa 86

Sharon Watts
201 Eastern Parkway #4K
Brooklyn, NY 11238

(718) 398-0451

Clients include:
The New York Times
Family Circle
Cosmopolitan
Good Housekeeping
Scholastic, Inc.
Welsh Publishing

Garison Weiland

(508) 362-7433

Clients include: IBM, NYNEX, *The Boston Globe, The Chicago Tribune, Harvard Business Review, Monitor, Runner's World, Technology Review, Walt Disney Adventures, Technology Review.*

ART STAFF, INC.

1000 JOHN R ROAD, SUITE 110
TROY, MICHIGAN 48083
1-800-526-0357
FAX: 1-313-583-4781

Art Staff, Inc. a full service art studio has been providing quality artwork to the advertising community for over thirty-five years. Artistic services are provided by a team of adept on-staff artists backed by experienced representation. As specialists in realistic illustration, we are equipped to handle the most challenging assignments.

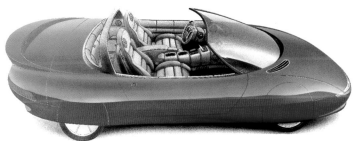

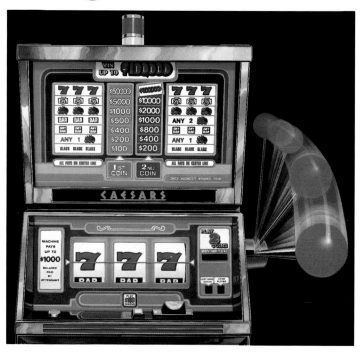

Sandy Nelson,
President

Joy Brosious
Larry Cory

Brian Foley
Jim Gutheil
Vicki Hayes
Ben Jaroslaw
Dan Kistler

John Martin
Dick Meissner
Gerry Monteleon
Linda Nagle
Jeff Ridky

Al Schrank
Ken Taylor
Peter Watson
Alan Wilson

PEGGY DRESSEL

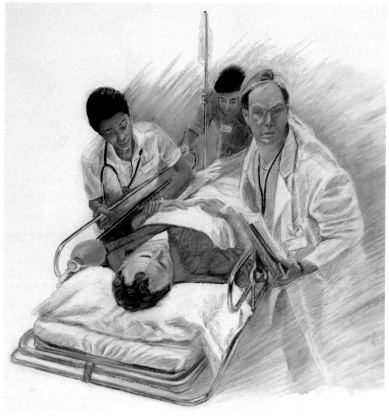

Clients include: *Blaircare Magazine*, Caribiner, CUC International, *Decision Magazine*, *Info World*, Macmillan/ McGraw-Hill School Publishing Co., Macy's, *MatureHealth*, *Medical Laboratory Observer*, OB/GYN, *The New York Doctor*, Vogue Patterns

11 ROCKAWAY AVENUE   OAKLAND, NJ 07436   201-337-2143

Thomas C. Duckworth

DUCKWORTH ILLUSTRATION INC.
10109 RAIN DROP CIRCLE
GRANGER, IN 46530

(219) 674-6226
FAX IN STUDIO

MAX

Max Seabaugh

Illustration

and Graphic Design

246 First Street

Suite 310

San Francisco

California 94105

Phone: 415/543.7775

Fax: 415/543.2431

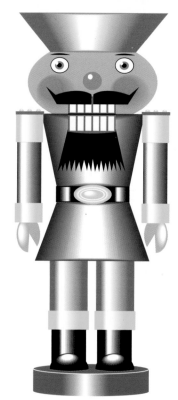

Illustrations created

on a Macintosh II

using Adobe Illustrator

ANTHONY A SIGALA

Tel/Fax 619 • 351 • 1880

657 Main Street
Ciudad Plaza
Brawley, California
92227

ILLUSTRATION

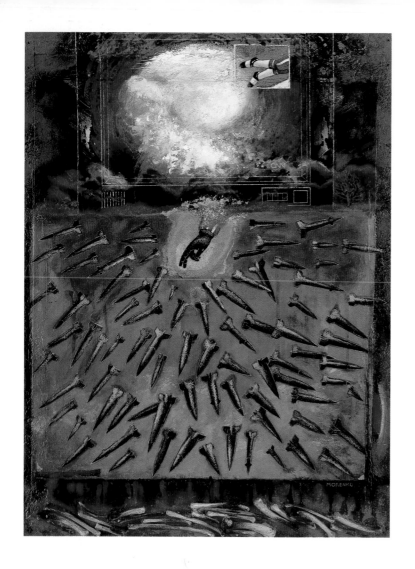

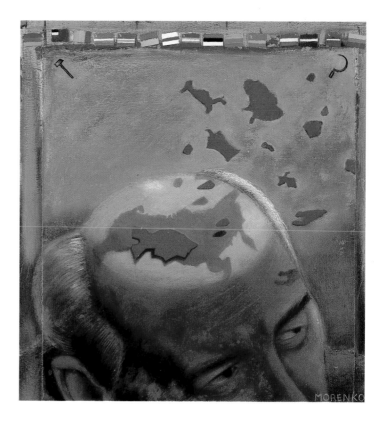

Michael Morenko
255 West 10th Street, Apt. 5FS
New York, New York 10014

(212) 627-5920

Clients: Botto, Rossner, Horne & Messinger (Ketchum Communications), Cliggott Communications, Maya Jones Imports, *Penthouse Magazine*.

Awards: Award of Excellence 1991 RX Club. Additional Credits: Art work accepted *American Illustration #11* (1992 Edition)

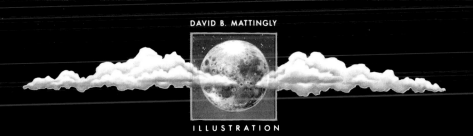

DAVID B. MATTINGLY

THE FINEST IN SCIENCE FICTION AND FANTASY ILLUSTRATION

201-659-7404

Jonathan Combs

Chateau Ste. Michelle

Spirit of Washington

Holland America

InterWest Savings

Sweet Represents

Ron Sweet **(415) 433-1222**

716 Montgomery Street, San Francisco, California 94111

Jonathan is represented in the Northwest by Pat Hackett (206) 447-1600

Anatoly

MEXICAN GOPHER TORTOISE

Gopherus flavomarginatus 15'6 inches

Ron Sweet **(415) 433-1222**

716 Montgomery Street, San Francisco, California 94111

So, what's your person?

Monet Changes Everything

Thom Donovan

HUMOROUS ILLUSTRATION
THE PIANO FACTORY
791 TREMONT STREET, E202
BOSTON, MA 02118

(617) 247-3237

Julia Gran
3240 Henry Hudson Parkway #6h
Riverdale, New York 10463

(718) 601-8820
Fax (718) 601-8266

Partial List of Clients:
• The Boston Globe
• Wall Street Journal
• Hearst Magazines
• Scholastic Inc.
• Continental Insurance
• Cosmopolitan Magazine

• The New York Times
• Leo Burnett Agency
• Institutional Investor Magazine
• Home Office Computing
  Magazine
• Diversions Magazine
• Louisville Magazine

• Town & Country Magazine
• Village Voice

Can also be seen in
Print Regional 1992

KEITH BATCHELLER

818/331-0439 FAX 818/331-4690
NEW YORK AMERICAN ARTISTS 212/682-2462

JEFF SEAVER

130 W 24TH ST #4B NY, NY 10011-1906 FAX 212/255-3823 PHONE 212/741-2279

Steve Voita

2202 E Flower Street
Phoenix, Arizona 85016

Phone & Fax (602) 956-7673

The flag went down, and Mike let his mind clear of everything except winning the race. He set off like a rocket and broke the lap record from a standing start, but Agostini was there as well and, although Mike put the lap record up to 108.7mph, Agostini's best lap was only a fraction slower.

Hailwood, frightened out of his wits by the combination of the big Honda and the TT circuit, was clearing spectators from walls and hedges all around the circuit with a frightening display of pitches, lurches and full-blown wheelies. Marshals along the Glen Helen section were reported to have leaped for cover convinced that the almost uncontrollable Honda was going to plough right into them. Over the limit though Mike was, he had to try even harder, for Ago posed a massive threat. To complicate matters, Hailwood's throttle kept coming off the handlebar. Frantic pit-stop activity with a mallet failed to cure the trouble, but Mike had no time to waste. It was the kind of stuff only heroes are

Steve Voita

2202 E FLOWER STREET

PHOENIX, ARIZONA 85016

PHONE & FAX (602) 956-7673

Ken Dallison

1282 Bramblewood Lane
Mississauga, Ontario
Canada L5H 1M1

Phone (416) 274-5594
Fax   (416) 274-7633

Member of the Society of Illustrators
Gold Medal

1928 Locomobile

1929 Pierce-Arrow

1931 Cord

Ken Dallison

1282 BRAMBLEWOOD LANE
MISSISSAUGA, ONTARIO
L5H 1M1 CANADA

PHONE & FAX (416) 274-7633

Born near London in 1933, Ken learned his basic trade at Twickenham Art College. He and his wife currently reside in Toronto wheere he works and occasionally teaches college level art. His highly regarded style has been a standard for the world of illustration.

Ken's work has adorned the pages of Esquire, National Geographic, Redbook, Sports Illustrated, Car & Driver, Road & Track, and Automobile magazines. In 1970, his illustrations for When Zeppelin Flew (Time-Life Books) brought him the Gold Medal

from the Society of Illustrators. Published in the Indy 500 program 1992.

FIONA  KING

3929 SANTA NELLA PLACE SAN DIEGO CA 92130

619 • 259 • 1400   FAX AVAILABLE

KOLLWITZ

KIM
FRALEY

PHONE OR FAX 619 727 3511

Pritchard Design
& Illustration

BRUCE A. PRITCHARD
5823 CRYSTAL SPRINGS HILL LANE
BAINBRIDGE IS., WA 98110

PHONE & FAX (206) 842-6788

Editorial

Humorous Editorial

Children's Illustration

Caricature

Cartooning

Graphic Design

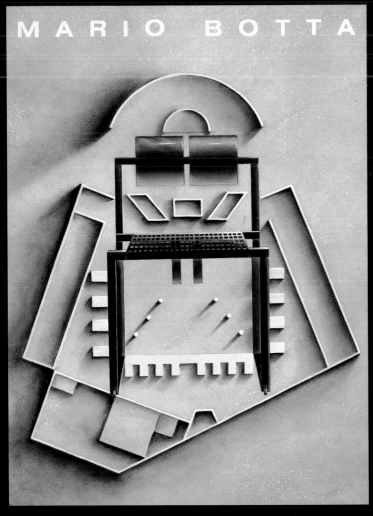

MARIO BOTTA

NEW STONE AGE

8403 WEST THIRD STREET · LOS ANGELES, CALIFORNIA 90048 · 213 · 658-9569

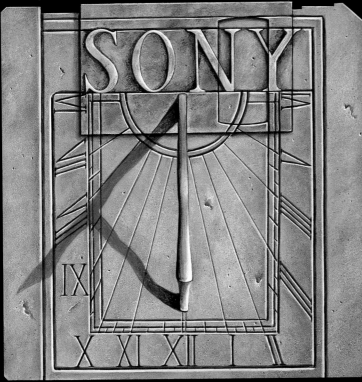

SONY

United Airlines   Annual Report 1990

Fred C. Smith
9024 E. ARCADIA AVENUE #A
SAN GABRIEL, CA 91775

(818) 291-2717
FAX (818) 291-2617

Editorial, advertising, product,
black & white.
Client list: NBC, Los Angeles Times,
U.C.L.A. Magazine, Stanford Magazine,
Vons, Pavilions, Stater Brothers,
Westways, California Business,
T.L. Enterprises.

Member: Society of Illustrators of
Los Angeles.

ROGER WHITE

212-362-1848   160 West End Ave. 3K   New York, N.Y. 10023
Represented by Creative Freelancers   212-398-9540

Sharon D. Siegel ✳ Illustration

47 Peyster Street • Albany • New York • 12208 • Phone/Fax 518•482•2336

THE ADVENTUROUS ILLUSTRATIONS OF TODD PEARL

ROBODUDE
PART MAN, PART MACHINE, TOTALLY *RAD*

PIRATE RADIO

RAD DOG SURF STICKS
"No Leash Required"

1616 BUTLER AVENUE • LOS ANGELES, CA 90025 • 310 473 4935 • FAX 310 473 6185

(Clockwise from top left) Robodude: T-shirt design, Pearl Design; Black Santa: greeting card, Pearl Design; Rad Dog: T-shirt design contest winner, Crazy Shirts Inc.; Party Pig: radio station promotion, KQLZ, Los Angeles.

RICHARD L. WEBER
WEBWORK ILLUSTRATION, INC.

CHICAGO
(312) 802.5343

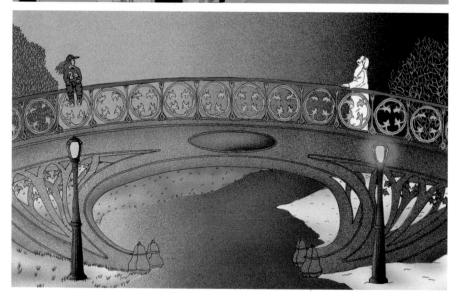

Juan Tenorio

830 AMSTERDAM AVENUE
NEW YORK, NY 10025

TEL: (212) 663-2626
FAX: (212) 663-3763

Macintosh computer
and fax in studio

Member Graphic Artists Guild

Clients have included:
The Chicago Tribune
The New York Times
Colgate Palmolive
Macmillan Publishing

Scholastic Magazine
Bantam Doubleday
Children's Television Workshop
MTV

"SAY CHEESE!"

Lisa Rauchwerger

CUTTING EDGE CREATIONS
8347 W. 4TH STREET
LOS ANGELES, CA 90048

PHONE & FAX (213) 651-2382

Specializing in papercut,
paper sculpture and cartoon
illustration, using watercolor
and calligraphy.

Member:
Society of Illustrators, Los Angeles
Society of Children's Book Writers

Barbara Rhodes

BARBARA RHODES ILLUSTRATION
6739 CANTIL STREET
LA COSTA, CALIFORNIA 92009

(619) 929-1049

Loose watercolor and/or pencil illustration featuring people, fashion, sports, landscape, product.
Clients include:
American Dairy Council, American Red Cross, CBS, Cleo/Gibson Greeting Cards, Inc., Culbertson Winery, *Dance Aerobics* Magazine, D.H. Technology, Golden Door Spa, Harcourt Brace Jovanovich, Inc., J.C. Penney, Kyocera International Inc., La Valencia Hotel, New American Library, *New York/ Newsday* Newspaper, Ordmark Development Company, Pacific Eyes & T's, Petite Sophisticate, Inc., Scripps Memorial Hospital, *Woman's World.*

See also: Graphic Artists Guild's Directory of Illustration Vol. 7 & 8.
Member: Society of Illustrators, San Diego; Graphic Artists Guild

CHARLES PEALE

IRONING JOHN

Clients include:
Children's Television Workshop
Entertainment Weekly
Modern Maturity
National Geographic Traveller

illustration
804-293-3394

National Wildlife
Playboy
Pulse!
U.S. News & World Report
Whittle Communications

Susan Swan

83 SAUGATUCK AVENUE
WESTPORT, CT 06880

(203) 226-9104
(203) 454-7956

Clients: Milton Bradley; Chemical Bank; McDougal, Littell & Co.; Delta SKY; MEDICAL ECONOMICS; CFO; Harcourt Brace Jovanovich; Scholastic; Houghton Mifflin; Holt Rinehart Winston; Doubleday Book & Music; Silver Burdett & Ginn; Macmillan/ McGraw Hill; Scott Foresman & Co., Harper Collins; Children's Television Workshop.

See also: Graphic Artists Guild Directory #5, 6, and 8; Corporate Showcase Vol. 10; American Showcase 15; The Creative Illustration Book 1992.

Member Graphic Artists Guild
©Susan Swan 1992

Michael Surles

MICHAEL SURLES ILLUSTRATOR
300 STONY POINT ROAD #191
SANTA ROSA, CA 95401

(707) 575-7367

San Francisco Society of Illustrators
Member

DOROTHEA SIERRA

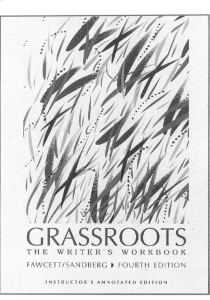

Dorothea Sierra
1 FITCHBURG STREET, #B252
SOMERVILLE, MA 02143

PHONE/FAX (617) 625-8070

Graphic illustration in gouache, cut paper, and line. Specializing in cultural and environmental work (animals—land and sea, plants, people and patterns) developed through travels, research and a highly developed color palette.

Work in publishing: children's books, covers and interior illustration. Consultant in conceptualization, color and design development.
Additional work in advertising, computer magazines and exhibit design, graphic symbols, marketing (award for series of promotional posters), promotional products: brochures, packaging, textiles, and cards.
Awards: New England Bookbuilders Cover Design 90 & 91; Print Magazine 91—Design Excellence for series cover design based on endangered animals.

PLAYTEX, INC.

TICKETRON, INC.
AWARD WINNING LOGO

OLAN LABS

ELIZABETH ARDEN

SEAGRAM'S

CHESEBROUGH POND'S

LIPTON, INC.

BLUE RIDGE FARMS, INC.

Fashion Shapers
PLAYTEX, INC.

CARLOTTA D'INGRES, LTD.

ETERNA '27
REVLON

ELIZABETH ARDEN

REVLON

TICKETRON

ELIZABETH ARDEN

Baldino Design
64 VERNON DRIVE
SCARSDALE, NY 10583

(914) 723-4001
Fax (914) 723-3544

Innovative
award
winning
designs.

Experience in solving
design problems for
leading art directors.

MARK & ERIN

SPARACIO

30 Rover Lane • Hicksville, NY 11801 • (516) 579-6679 • Fax (516) 735-8474

Represented by Wendy Morgan Network Studios (516) 757-5609 Fax (516) 261-6584

Robert Crawford

123 MINORTOWN ROAD
WOODBURY, CT 06798

(203) 266-0059

Robert Crawford graduated with a BFA from Rhode Island School of Design in 1975. His acrylic paintings have appeared in the *SI Annual, CA, Graphis,* and *Print* and he is a member of the Society of Illustrators. He has had group shows in New York, Japan and Germany and resides in Woodbury, Connecticut with his wife and two children. Among his clients are Volkswagen, Avon Books, *Fortune,* British Petroleum, Penguin USA, IBM, *The Atlantic,* Bantam Books, Pentagram, Harper Collins, Alfa Romeo, *U.S. News & World Report* and Random House.

CALL EVERETT DAVIDSON 914/693-7121

A partial client list includes: General Foods, Post Cereals, Nestle, Newsweek,
Golf Digest & Tennis Magazines, Burger King, Home Box Office,
Delmonte, Playboy Circulation and Lufthansa Airlines.

I can fax black and white copies of my portfolio to you on request.

Ask to be put on my mailing list.

STRAIGHT ARROW STUDIOS • 26 Parkway Drive, Dobbs Ferry, N.Y. 10522

...Take the High road!

Bot Roda

78 Victoria Lane
Lancaster, PA 17603

Phone & Fax (717) 393-1406

Humorous Illustration for Editorial,
Advertising and Corporate usage.
Member Society of Illustrators.
Work can also be seen in Humor 2,
RSVP 15 and American Showcase 14.
Client list available.
Portfolio available on request.

SUSAN PIZZO 914·664·4423

SMALL PRESS
THE MAGAZINE OF INDEPENDENT PUBLISHING
SPRING 1992 $5.95

▶ BOOGIE DOWN AT THE ABA
▶ HOW TO GET REVIEWED IN THE NY TIMES
▶ SELLING OFF YOUR RIGHTS -- FOR PROFIT
▶ BEAN COUNTING 101
PLUS
JEANNE DUPRAU   SALLIE BINGHAM
LENORA CHAMPAGNE   **ROBERTO JUARROZ**
PAUL PINES   LINDA NIEMANN

MARYLAND
LIVE

NEW COKE

S.PIZZO

STUDIO PIZZO OR PIZZO 288 E. DEVONIA AVE. MT. VERNON, N.Y. 10552
CLIENTS INCLUDE: ADWEEK • ASSOCIATED PRESS • THE BALTIMORE SUN • BARRON'S • THE BOSTON GLOBE • COCA-COLA •
CONDE NAST • COSMOPOLITAN • FAMILY CIRCLE • MACMILLAN PUBLISHING • MACY'S • McCANN-ERICKSON • RANDOM HOUSE •
KNOPF BOOKS • SOUTHERN COMFORT • TIME, INC. • THE WASHINGTON POST • WINSTON-SALEM • Y&R/BRAVO GROUP
MORE WORK: ADWEEK PORTFOLIO OF ILLUSTRATION '88 • GRAPHIC ARTIST'S GUILD DIRECTORY OF ILLUSTRATION 6
CALL ANYTIME FOR SAMPLES OR PORTFOLIO!

STUDIO PIZZO OR PIZZO 288 E. DEVONIA AVE. MT. VERNON, N.Y. 10552

CLIENTS INCLUDE: AMERICAN EXPRESS • CHASE • COCA-COLA • COLUMBIA PICTURES TELEVISION • EASTERN AIRLINES • LETRASET •
MACY'S • NEWSWEEK • NORWEGIAN CRUISE LINE • N.Y. TIMES • PIONEER • PRODIGY • TEXACO • TIME INC. • U.S. ARMY
MORE WORK/AWARDS: ADWEEK PORTFOLIOS '88 • SHOWCASE 12 • N.Y. GOLD 3,4 • CONCEPTUAL ILLUSTRATION 1 • PRINT '88, '90, '91
• GRAPHIS DESIGN '91 • CREATIVITY '91 • OZZIE SILVER '91 • HOW '89 • AR100 '89 • SPD 23, 25, 27, • SPOTS '87 • SND12 • DESI 12

C A L L   A N Y T I M E   F O R   S A M P L E S   O R   P O R T F O L I O !

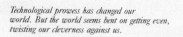
Technological prowess has changed our world. But the world seems bent on getting even, twisting our cleverness against us.

REVENGE THEORY

by EDWARD TENNER

Why are the lines at automatic cash dispensers longer in the evening than those at tellers' windows used to be during banking hours? Why do helmets and other protective gear help make football more dangerous than rugby? Why do filter-tip cigarettes usually fail to reduce nicotine intake? Why are today's paperback prices starting to overtake yesterday's cloth-bound prices? Why has the leisure society gone the way of the leisure suit?

The world we have created seems to be getting even, twisting our cleverness against us. Or we may be the ones who are unconsciously twisting. Either way, wherever we turn we face the ironic unintended consequences of mechanical, chemical, medical, social, and financial ingenuity—revenge effects, they might be called.

Revenge effects don't require space-age technology. As the humorist Will Cuppy observed of the first pyramids, "Imhotep the Wise originated the idea of concealing the royal corpse and his treasure in a monument so conspicuous that it could not possibly be missed by body snatchers and other thieves." At Elizabethan hangings of cutpurses, their surviving colleagues worked the distracted throngs.

Cognizance of revenge effects is much more recent. Craftworkers and farmers before the nineteenth century, as far as I can tell, didn't seem to blame their tools or materials when things went wrong. They recognized providence and luck, and some of them (notably miners) discerned malicious spirits, but not ornery ordinary *things.* For all the prophecy of Mary Shelley and the insight of Henry David Thoreau, the critic Friedrich Theodor Vischer (1807-1887) probably deserves the honor of propelling revenge theory into common speech in a novel, *Auch Einer (Another)*, published in 1867. His eccentric—critics say, autobiographical—hero is convinced that everyday objects, like pencils, pens, inkwells, and cigars, harbor a perverse and demonic spirit. Although not quite in today's literary canon even in his native Germany, Vischer did achieve immortality through the phrase *die Tücke des Objekts*—the malice of things.

In 1878 Thomas Edison, possibly echoing telegraphers' slang, first wrote of a *bug* as a hidden problem to be removed from a design. According to a later article in *The Pall Mall Gazette*, he was implying "that some imaginary insect has secreted itself inside and is causing all the trouble." It appears that by the mid-1930s, "ironing the bugs out" had become American engineering slang.

By the 1940s the complexity of technological systems raised the consciousness of troops and civilians alike about how many things could go wrong. The London *Observer* acknowledged in 1942 that the behavior of machines "couldn't always be explained by . . . laws of aerodynamics. And so, lacking a Devil, the young fliers . . . invented a whole hierarchy of devils. They called them Gremlins. . . . "

In 1949 revenge theory took a giant step when Col. P. J. Stapp of Edwards Air Force Base referred to (his colleague Captain Ed) Murphy's Law—that if something can go wrong, it will—in a press conference. Aeronautical manufacturers soon were exploiting it in their advertising, and it passed into folklaw, that vast body of free-form theorizing. Only a year

B R I A N
LIES
(617)876-0678

9 HUMBOLDT STREET
CAMBRIDGE, MA 02140

CLIENTS INCLUDE:
BOSTON GLOBE
CHRISTIAN SCIENCE MONITOR
HOUGHTON MIFFLIN CO.
LITTLE, BROWN & CO.
LA TIMES SYNDICATE
HARVARD MAGAZINE
CRICKET
LADYBUG
LOTUS
BOSTON BUSINESS
INVESTMENT VISION
PC WEEK
TECHNOLOGY REVIEW
NEW ENGLAND BUSINESS

P.RAT DESIGN

Russell E. Pratt
Studio 201-863-8227

Lettering • Design and Illustration for Packaging and Advertising

© Russell Pratt 1992 • Member Graphic Artist Guild

Janet Pietrobono   Member Graphic Artists Guild

5 SPRING STREET
MOUNT KISCO, NEW YORK 10549

(914) 666-4730

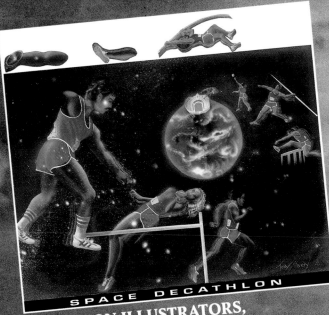

SPACE DECATHLON

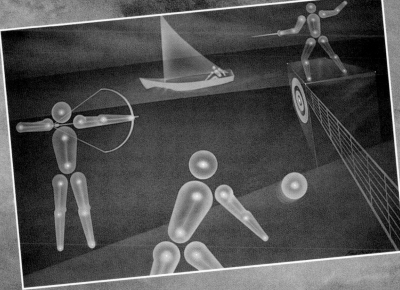

ATTENTION ILLUSTRATORS, PUBLISHERS & AD AGENCIES

There is a new technology available to create flat movement to one or many parts of an ad, P.O.P. or poster–without motors! Using motion sensors, movement occurs when you approach the piece. The illustration above shows how a motion poster is painted. The parts on top will be die-cut & placed into its moving position. From fine art to advertising, this technology is movin'.
Call for details.

Tony Avery
9855 Jamaica Circle
Huntington Beach, CA
92646
(714)962-8862
Fax(714)968-6130

T O M   L O C H R A Y

REPRESENTED IN THE EAST BY JILL KAHN [612] 925-1699

REPRESENTED IN THE WEST BY RON SWEET [415] 433-1222

REPRESENTED IN CHICAGO BY DAN SELL [312] 565-2701

Jim Roldan
141 E. Main Street
E. Hampstead, NH 03826

Phone & Fax (603) 382-1686

Illustrations created for: AAA, Banyan Systems, Boston Magazine, Brookside Hospital, Byte Magazine, Carpet One, Computer Graphics World, Consolidated Group Trust, Cabletron, Data General, Don Law Concerts, Frye Boots, Heinle & Heinle, Itek Corporation, Lapham/Miller Associates, Jolicoeur Publications, New Hampshire Heart Institute, P3 Magazine, White Mountain Graphics, among others.

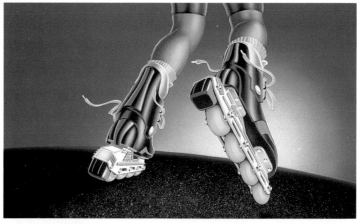

Rob Hess

63 LITTLEFIELD ROAD
EAST GREENWICH, RHODE ISLAND 02818

(401) 885-0331
FAX IN STUDIO

Technical and realistic illustration, rendered from blueprints, photographic references or product samples. Services include color, B&W photo retouching.

Clients include: American Tourister, AT&T, Colibri, DCA, Dexter Shoes, Euro-Disney, Hewlett-Packard, Keds, Marriott–Copley Place, Metropolitan Life, North Safety Equipment, Stratus Computers.

Additional samples in American Showcase Volumes 12, 13, 14, 15.

Member Graphic Artists Guild
© 1992 Rob Hess

Viv Eisner-Hess

63 Littlefield Road
East Greenwich, Rhode Island 02818

(401) 884-3424
Fax (401) 885-0331

Portfolio and client list available upon request.

Member Graphic Artists Guild
© 1992 Viv Eisner-Hess

JEFFERY HITCH

INDIANAPOLIS 500

DOC WAYNE'S MEDICINE SHOW

MEGUIARS WAX

ROCK BOTTOM BREWERY / FALCON PALE ALE

NORDIK WOLF BEER

J.L. Hitch/Illustration   4500 Campus Drive, Suite 692, Newport Beach, CA 92660   (714) 250-8640
Represented in Denver by: Paulette Rhyne Artist/Rep (303) 871-9166

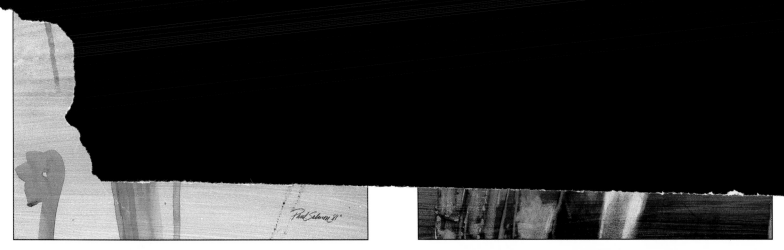

Paul Salmon

5826 Jackson's Oak Ct.
Burke, VA 22015

(703) 250-4943
Fax (703) 425-4565
© Paul Salmon 1992

Clients:
NASA
Time-Life Books
The National Air & Space Museum
Air & Space Smithsonian
National Geographic Society
Mobil Oil

American Forces Information Services
U.S. Department of Labor
Food & Drug Administration
U.S. Postal Service
The Washington Post

Awards:
Art Directors Club of Washington
Art Directors Club of New York
Society of Illustrators
Illustrators Club of Washington, DC
Virginia Commonwealth University
    Alumni Award in Design

Russell Gundlach

R. Gundlach Illustrations
51-11 72 Street
Woodside, NY 11377

(718) 424-1305

MFA Illustration School of Visual Arts

Member of Graphic Artists Guild

Marc Rosenthal

#8 ROUTE 66
MALDEN BRIDGE, NY 12115

(518) 766-4191
FAX (518) 766-4191

Clients include:
Altman & Manley/Eagle Advertising,
Fortune, Time, Newsweek, U.S. News
& World Report, Playboy, New York
Magazine, Vanity Fair, AT&T, Whittle
Communications, The Boston Globe,

The Washington Post, The New York
Times, The Philadelphia Inquirer.

THE X JOURNAL MAGAZINE

EATING WELL MAGAZINE

Jude Maceren

92 KOSSUTH STREET
PISCATAWAY, NEW JERSEY 08854

PHONE & FAX (908) 752-5931

Partial client list:
Sigs Publication/*The X Journal, C++ Report; Eating Well; Sacramento;* The Courier-News.
Work can also be seen in: *Graphic Artists Guild's Directory of Illustration 8* (1992 edition), page 113.

Member Graphic Artists Guild
©Jude Maceren 1992

Bradley O. Pomeroy

932 S. Walter Reed Drive #2
Arlington, Virginia 22204

(703) 920-7765
Fax in studio

A little humor, a little romance and a lot of life are the stuff this work is made of. There is no line between fine art and illustration—rather a marriage of the two.

Clients include: Time-Life Music; National Geographic Society; AT&T; C&P Telephone Co.; Wolf Trap Farm Park; National Humane Society; Environmental Protection Agency.

Simpson Paper Company

The Boston Globe

New York Magazine

Stanford (Published by Stanford Alumni Association)

Tim Lewis   184 St. Johns Place   Brooklyn, NY   11217   718 857-3406   Fax: 398-3788

Roger Jones

ROGER JONES · ILLUSTRATOR
34 GORHAM STREET
CAMBRIDGE, MA 02138

(617) 661-8645

Gold Medal
SILA

ERIC **REESE** / ILLUSTRATION

1023 Prospect Ave., #6. Long Beach, CA 90804

3 1 0 - 4 3 8 - 8 9 7 7 • F a x i n S t u d i o

North Bridge Group

RM&D Advertising

R&R Advertising

Frank Schulwolf Co.

NAV Press

ANIMATION REEL ON REQUEST

JARED D. LEE
(513)932-2154
2942 Hamilton Road / Lebanon, Ohio 45036

PORTFOLIO FOLDER AVAILABLE
FAX (513)932-9389

Rebecca Perry

Phone/Fax/Modem (212) 534-6204
220 E. 95th St., New York, New York 10128

LISTEN TO SNOW CLOSINGS ON B104. YOU COULD WIN SOME COLD CASH.

Next time it snows, you could earn a lot of money without ever picking up a shovel. Just listen to B104.

B104 announces snow closings and delayed openings at least four times an hour. And we give away $1,004 on the air, every time school's cancelled for the whole day.

So if you want to know if school's closed due to snow, tune into Baltimore's Best. And win some cold cash from the hot one . . . B104.

BALTIMORE'S BEST

B104 MEANS MUSIC.

Liquid Assets.

Sometimes life's little surprises can leave you feeling like you're really up a creek. That's why you need Chec-King, a convenient line of credit that you can use whenever and wherever you need it.

Fill out a credit application just once, and you'll be able to access your line by writing a check from your regular checkbook in the amount you need above your current checking balance. Chec-King will automatically cover that portion so it's an instant loan *and* overdraft protection.

And for those times when only cash will do, you can use any Carroll County Bank, MOST or Plus system automatic teller machine.

Chec-King can be used with any of Carroll County Bank's checking accounts, which offer you the benefits of Carroll County Bank's longer hours,

convenient locations and reliable, knowledgeable service. So whether you have an account with us, or plan to open one in the future, you'll want to request Chec-King.

Keep life's little surprises in check. With Chec-King.

CARROLL COUNTY BANK AND TRUST COMPANY

MEMBER FDIC

Scott Mattern

2229 NORTH CHARLES STREET
BALTIMORE, MARYLAND 21218

(410) 467-2639
FAX (410) 467-1869

Clients include: Macmillan, Black & Decker, Noxell, USF&G, Nestlé, W.B. Doner, *Baltimore Sun*, Johns Hopkins Health System.

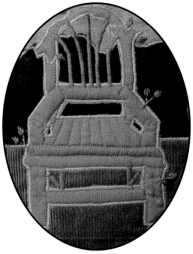

Deborah Keats

23 Washington Avenue
Schenectady, NY 12305

(518) 382-7560 (Phone/Fax)

Dimensional illustration using fabric, stitching and found objects.

Photography of the work is included.

Member: Graphic Artists Guild

For additional work see:
American Showcase Illustration 16

Michelle Lester

15 WEST 17TH STREET 9TH FLOOR
NEW YORK, NY 10011

PHONE: (212) 989-1411
FAX: (212) 627-8553

Distinctive Illustration in waterbased media, airbrush, pastel and pencil (color and b/w); mural and carpet fantasy environments, and interior rendering.

Clients include:
Saatchi & Saatchi Worldwide, Courtaulds Fibres Ltd., Dalton & Dalton Architects, Key Pharmaceuticals, Airco Corporation, Thompson-McKinnon, 3M Company, Neiman Marcus, Prudential Insurance Co., Marshall Field, New York Power Authority, Honeywell, Inc., Metropolitan Life, Sheraton Grande Tokyo, General Electric, Allied Dept. Stores, Bonwit Teller, FCB/Leber Katz Partners, Syracuse China, Ciner Manufacturing Co.
Member Graphic Artists Guild

Patrick Kelley

"Illustrations with the Right Touch"
1127 California
Grand Rapids, MI 49504

(616) 459-7540

Additional illustrations may be seen
in GAG Directory of Illustration #8

Member Graphic Artists Guild
Society of Children's Book Writers

Terry Boles

REPRESENTED BY

GLORIA BLOCKEY/CREATIVE NETWORK

3313 CROFT DRIVE

MINNEAPOLIS, MN 55418

(612) 781-7385   FAX (612) 781-2333

All kinds of really good illustration!
Terry Boles repped by
Gloria Blockey/Creative Network,
illustration, design, photography
& writing resource.

Norman
RAINOCK
804·264·8123

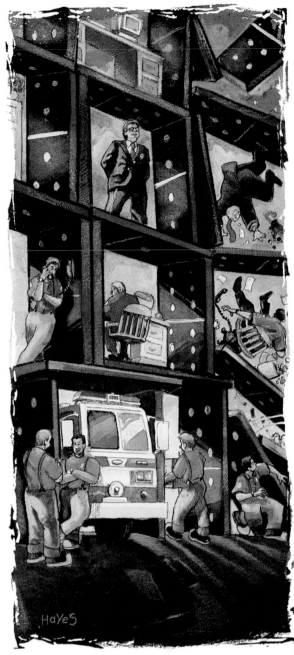

Josh Hayes

Stormship Studios
661 Massachusetts Avenue
Arlington, MA 02174

Phone: (617) 646-9517
Fax: (617) 646-3623

STORMSHIP
STUDIOS

Clients Include:

Bose Corporation, *Boston Magazine*, Brown Publishing Network,
Cahners Publishing, Charrette Corporation, CMC Advertising,
Computer World Magazine, DC Heath, Digital, the Environmental
Protection Agency, Fidelity Investments, *Honolulu Magazine*,
Houghton Mifflin Company, Lotus Publishing, NFPA Journal

☎

414 - 692 - 9354

North 6259 Highway I, Fredonia, Wisconsin 53021

"We forget that the beauty of an opening rose can make our hearts open."

-Susan Griffin

JOHN ERIC KARPINSKI

California Archaeology Week

John A. Lytle

LYTLE STUDIO
17130 YOSEMITE ROAD
P.O. BOX 5155
SONORA, CA 95370

PHONE & FAX (209) 928-4849

Additional illustrations may be seen in American Showcase 5–7, 10–16; Art Directors Index 10, 11; Adweek Portfolio 1986; GAG Directory of Illustration 5, 7, 8.
Clients include: ABC Sports, American Express, AT&T, Bank of America, CBS Sports, Edelbrock, Eli Lilly, Goodyear, Hewlett Packard, Jaguar, Levi-Strauss, Nike, New York Telephone, NFL Films, PG&E, Reebok, R.J. Reynolds, Ryder Trucks, Seagrams, Sheraton, Sperry, Sports Illustrated, Squirt, Visa, Yamaha Motorcycles.

Member: Society of Illustrators, Graphic Artists Guild

New Methods, Old Attitudes

Wall Street

David Gothard

(215) 588-4937
Fax (215) 588-4943

Clients include:
Asia Inc., AT&T, Barnett Design, Business Tokyo, Business Week, Children's TV Workshop, Deutch Design, Emergency Medicine, Financial World, IBM, International Business, International Herald Tribune, Kettering Foundation, Los Angeles Times, New York, New York Times, Oxford University Press, Philadelphia, Public Agenda Foundation, Time, Town & Country, Travel Holiday, Wall Street Journal, Warkulwiz Design, Washington Post.

KATHERINE MAHONEY *Illustrations*

617·868·7877
617·489·0406

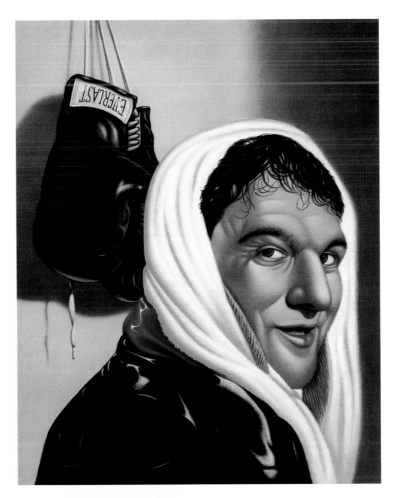

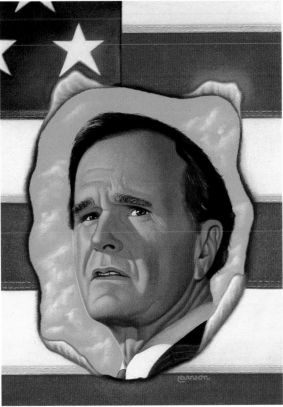

David Levinson
219-D RICHFIELD TERRACE
CLIFTON, NEW JERSEY 07012

PHONE & FAX (201) 614-1627

Clients include: Alfred A. Knopf, American Tobacco Company, Better Health, Cable Marketing, CBS Records, Circle K, Communications Consultant, Doubleday Books & Music Club, Dutton Children's Books, Gallery, Inside Sports, Kiwanis International, Medical Economics, New York Times, R.N., Scholastic Inc., 20/20, U.S. Pharmacist, View, Writers Digest.

Society of Illustrators Annual 29, 30 and 33
Member of the Graphic Artists Guild

Judith Sutton

239 Dean Street
Brooklyn, NY 11217

718 • 834 • 8851

Judith Sutton

239 Dean Street
Brooklyn, NY 11217

718 • 834 • 8851

Doree Loschiavo (signature)

Doree Loschiavo
2714 S. Marvine Street
Philadelphia, PA 19148

(215) 336-1724

Member:
Graphic Artists Guild
National Artists Equity
Midwest Watercolor Society
Catharine Lorillard Wolfe Art Club
Philadelphia Watercolor Club

Clients include:
World Cycling Ltd., Subaru, Philadelphia Stock Exchange, Philadelphia Electric Company, Philadelphia Convention and Visitors Bureau, Woman's Day Magazine, The American University, Baltimore Magazine, National

Multiple Sclerosis Society Cycling Classic.
Illustration and design creating a strong emotional response to the color, energy and motion of her subjects.
Slide portfolio available.

Michael McGurl

14 Garbosa Road

Santa Fe, NM 87505

(505) 986-5889

Fax (505) 982-8253

"A mind that is stretched to a new idea never returns to its original dimension."

—Oliver Wendell Holmes

ILLUSTRATION DESIGN

PAM-ELA HARRELSON

2707 BEECHMONT DR.

DALLAS TEXAS 75228

TEL   214 - 321 - 6061

FAX   214 - 321 - 7424

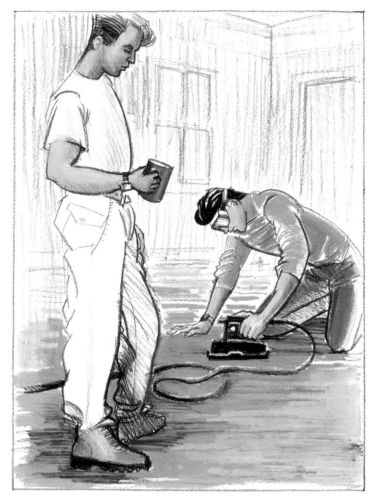

Hugh Harrison

314 Pavonia Avenue
Jersey City, NJ 07302

(201) 798-6086

Member Graphic Artists Guild

gumble
i l l u s t r a t i o n

Gary Gumble

803 ELMWOOD AVENUE
EVANSTON, IL 60202

(708) 475-4712   FAX AVAILABLE
IN MINNEAPOLIS CALL:
DIANE ROGERS (612) 339-7055

Without art, the crudeness of reality
would make the world unbearable.
(George Bernard Shaw)

Donna Ingemanson

36 South Franklin Street
Holbrook, MA 02343

(617) 767-3007
Fax in Studio
Answering Service (617) 734-8494

Effective illustrations with a unique twist.

Experienced in all medias.

BRAD HAMANN

330 WESTMINSTER ROAD BROOKLYN, NY 11218 • 718-287-6086 • FAX 718-826-6113

TOM GRAHAM
(718) 680-2975

PARTIAL LIST OF CLIENTS:
The New York Times, LIFE Magazine, Arcade Publishing, E.P. Dutton, Henry Holt, TIME-LIFE, Saatchi & Saatchi,
E.B. Wilson Agency, The Wine Spectator, Oxford University Press

Bob Eggleton

Bob Eggleton Illustration
P.O. Box 5692
Providence, RI 02903 USA

(401) 831 5030

Clients include:

Bantam/Doubleday/Dell, Berkley Publishing Group, Warner Books, TSR Inc., TOR Books, Massa International/Ultra Co. Ltd.

Above images Copyright© Bob Eggleton. Godzilla character & Super X copyright© Toho Ltd.

KEN GRANING, 1975 CRAGIN DR. BLOOMFIELD HILLS, MI 48302. (313) 851-3665 FAX: (313) 851-1828

Ron McKee

RON MCKEE STUDIOS
32362 LAKE PLEASANT DRIVE
WESTLAKE VILLAGE, CA 91361

(818) 889-6692

Paintings for
individual and
corporate clients
for fine art and
advertising.

Gary Ferster

57 WEST END AVENUE
LONG BRANCH, NJ 07740

(908) 229-5774

Macintosh® Computer Illustration

Member Graphic Artists Guild

Abe Gurvin

FESTIVE ILLUSTRATIONS FOR ALL OCCASIONS
31341 HOLLY DRIVE
LAGUNA BEACH, CA 92677

(714) 499-2001 (STUDIO & FAX)

N.Y.: Tricia Weber (212) 799-6532
S.F.: Freda Scott (415) 621-2992
ATLANTA: The Williams Group
(404) 873-2287
L.A.: Fox & Spencer (213) 653-6484
CHICAGO: Joel Harlib (312) 329-1370

David Graves

160 W. 24TH STREET APT. 5M
NEW YORK, NY 10011

(212) 463-9354
FAX IN STUDIO

Images and lettering for advertising,
corporate, and publishing usage.

Member:
Society of Illustrators
Graphic Artists Guild

© David Graves

Rob Dunlavey

8 FRONT STREET
NATICK, MA 01760

(508) 651-7503
(508) 651-8344 FAX

B.A. FRIEDMAN

29 BANK ST. STUDIO TEL 212 ▪ 242 ▪ 4951 **NY NY 10014**

CLIENTS INCLUDE: ADWEEK ▪ THE AMERICAN SPECTATOR ▪ THE ATLANTIC
ILLINOIS STATE MEDICAL SOCIETY ▪ THE NEW YORK TIMES ▪ SCHOLASTIC
TENNIS MAGAZINE ▪ U.S. NEWS & WORLD REPORT ▪ WEIGHT WATCHERS

Colin Poole
I L L U S T R A T I O N

817 Mackall Avenue, McLean, Virginia 22101   Telephone (703) 893-0759   Fax (703) 448-1270

LINA CHESAK ◆ ILLUSTRATION

2265 Idylwood Station Lane, Falls Church, Virginia 22043   Tel: 703/573-4230

Vala Kondo

230 WEST 79TH STREET #52
NEW YORK, NY 10024

(212) 517-4052

Clients include:
Adweek, American Health Posters, Barrons, *The Boston Globe,* Business Week, California Magazine, Entertainment Weekly, Forbes, Global Finance, InCider, Inc., Kiplingers Magazine, *The Los Angeles Times,* Money Magazine,

Muscle & Fitness, Network Computing, *The New York Times,* New Woman, Shape Magazine, *The Wall Street Journal, The Washington Post,* U.S. News & World Report

Robbin Gourley

ILLUSTRATION

244 FIFTH AVENUE 11TH FLOOR
NEW YORK, NEW YORK 10001

PHONE (212) 966-4048
FAX   (212) 679-9422

Steve Jenkins

ILLUSTRATION
244 FIFTH AVENUE 11TH FLOOR
NEW YORK, NEW YORK 10001

PHONE (212) 679-9430
FAX (212) 679-9422

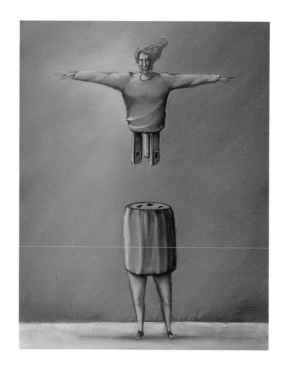

Ken Dubrowski

Portfolio available on request

KEN DUBROWSKI ILLUSTRATION
49 FREEMAN STREET
WOLLASTON, MA 02170

PHONE & FAX (617) 328-1198

© WALT DISNEY CO.

© WALT DISNEY CO.

Mike Dietz
P.O. Box 3145
San Clemente, CA 92677

(714) 496-3021

Member Graphic Artists Guild.
Fax in studio.

John Paul Genzo

ILLUSTRATION
802 RAVENS CREST DRIVE
PLAINSBORO, NJ 08536

(609) 275-5601
FAX (609) 799-8707

Clients include: American Journal of Nursing, Carol & Graff Publishing, Chelsea House Publishing, Citibank, Digital Computers, Fidelity Investments, Harcourt, Brace, Jovanovich Publications, HarperCollins Publishing, Hospital Practice Publishing Company, Inter-Governmental Philatelic Corporation, Ketchum Advertising, Marketing, Communication Systems Inc., McGraw-Hill, National Review Magazine, The New Republic Magazine, Penguin Books Canada, Pennsylvania Hospital, Public Relations Journal, Saint Michael's Medical Center, Scholastic Books, Sea World, G.D. Searle & Company, Springhouse Corporation, Sunkist, World Health Communications. Member Graphic Artists Guild.

See also GAG's Dir. of Illustration #8, The Creative Illustration Book 1991

©JOHN PAUL GENZO

What do men fear?

...not Dan V. Romer 176 Fifth Avenue...
Brooklyn, N.Y. 11217 apt. 4R telephone...
718-189-8442. for client lists see Graphic
Artist Guild Directories 5-8. (above illustration done
for Ladies Home Journal.)

Jack McConnell

McConnell McNamara & Company
182 Broad Street
Wethersfield, CT 06109

(203) 563-6154
Fax (203) 563-6159

Photo illustrations . . . polaroid image transfers painted with pastels, water-colors and oils. It all begins with a photograph. One of 150,000 images in Jack McConnell's stock photo library . . . or something new to satisfy your imagination and meet your project objectives. Subjects already on file—landscapes, environmental, nature, nautical, sports, music, games, food, Americana, families, children, elderly, lifestyle concepts, social issues, business themes, energy, healthcare, global markets, occupations like farming, ranching, orchards, construction, transportation, office, retail, finance, manufacturing, industrial. For annual reports, brochures, advertising, packaging, calendars, greeting cards, posters, editorials, book covers, and exhibition art.

SUSAN DETRICH · ILLUSTRATION

SUSAN DETRICH · 253 Baltic Street · Brooklyn New York 11201 · 718-237-9174

Also see the Graphic Artists Guild's Directory of Illustration 5, 6, 8, the Creative Illustration Book 1991 & RSVP 16, 17, 18

David Dennis Masse 215 494 7525 *ILLUSTRATION* 81 Seward Lane Aston PA 19014

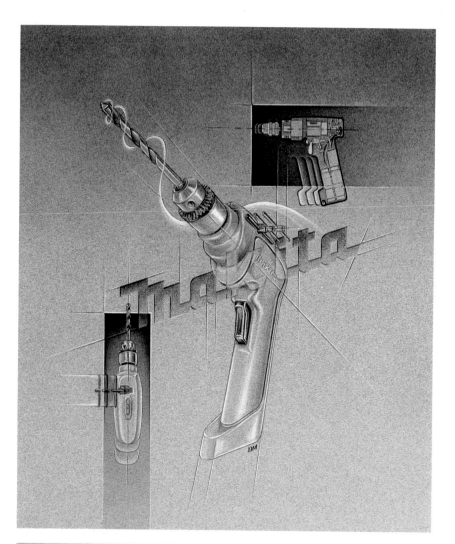

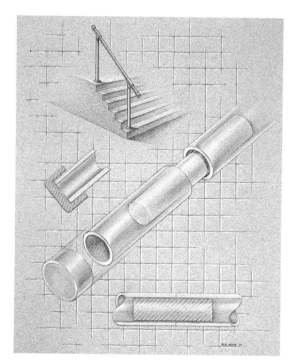

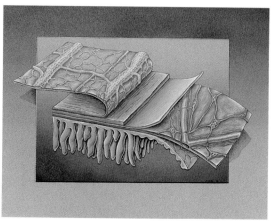

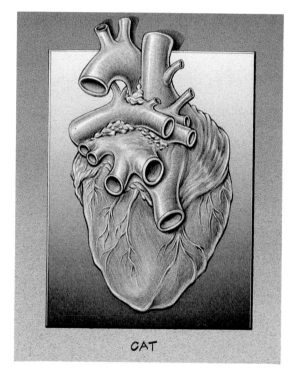

CAT

Clients include:

Citibank, Honeywell, DuPont, Rouse, Ketchum, LGK, Franklin Mint, Westinghouse, Scott Paper, ARCO, McGraw Hill, W.B. Saunders, Harcourt Brace Jovanovich, Philadelphia Inquirer

FAX: 215-494-7525 Member Graphic Artists Guild ©1992 David Dennis Masse

DANIEL ABRAHAM

718 • 499 • 4006

Box 2528 Rockefeller Center Station
New York, New York 10185
Fax in Studio
Deliveries:
425 Fifth Avenue
Brooklyn, New York 11215

I'll draw you funny folks in color
or in black and white;
I'll do it with a long lead time,
or do it overnight.

For books or ads or magazines,
or corporate profiles,
or any other place you need
a message with a smile.

Clients include:
Chicago Tribune, Forbes, Governing,

Hadassah, *Newsweek, New York Times,
New York Daily News,* Nickelodeon,
NYLIC, Oxford University Press,
Random House, Reader's Digest Books,
Scholastic, *Ski,* Sony, *Spy,* TIAA-CREF,
University of Chicago Press,
Washington Post.

SUSAN HUNT YULE
ILLUSTRATION
(212) 226-0439
日本 03-3490-8231

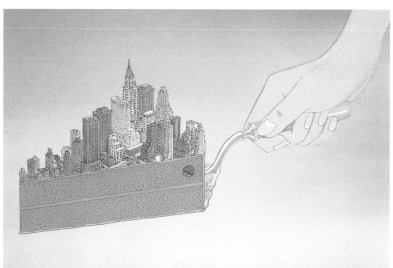

© SUSAN HUNT YULE.1992

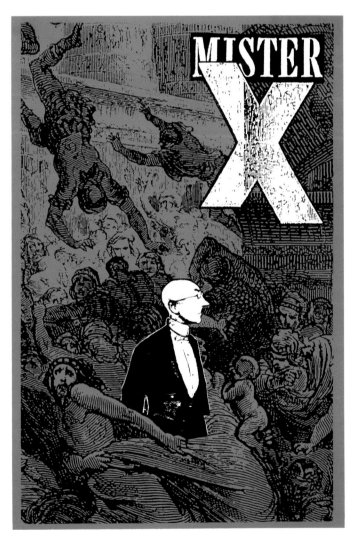

Matthew Johnson

ILLUSTRATOR
(212) 865-9447

354 W. 110th Street Apt. 3A
New York City, NY 10025

Douglas Andelin
(415) 927-1057

Boston Magazine

Douglas Andelin
(415) 927-1057

D E B R A · S · H A R D E S T Y

1017 Vallejo Way   Sacramento, CA 95818   TEL 916·446·1824   FAX 916·446·5661

THOMAS AMOROSI

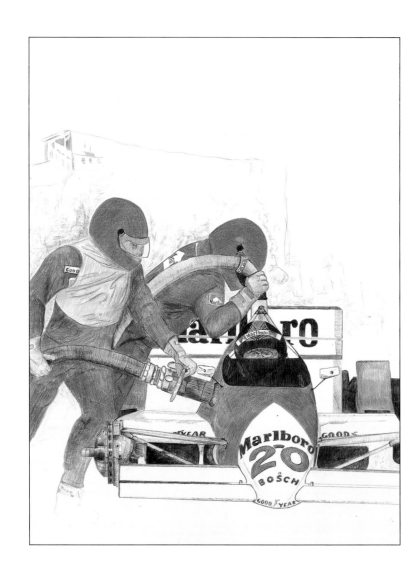

TERESA AMOROSI

homas Amorosi
eresa Amorosi

NTAGLIO DIMENSION

COMPTON STREET

AST ROCKAWAY, NY 11518

TUDIO: TEL./FAX: (516) 596-0160

MESSAGES: (516) 593-3845

Color and Black & White conceptual,
editorial, juvenile, medical/scientific
illustration. Work appears in American
Showcase 14 & 15, Illustrators 33,
Directory of Illustration #8 and the 4th
& 5th editions of AMI source book.

Affiliations:
Graphic Artists Guild
Association of Medical Illustrators
Guild of Natural Science Illustrators

Clients:
North Atlantic Bio-Cultural
   Organization
Hunter College, CUNY
Kids Work, Child & Adolescent
   Therapy
MLS Learning Center

MARK A. BENDER ▪ 930 NORTH LINCOLN AVE. ▪ PITTSBURGH, PA 15233 ▪ (412) 321-3266

The Azmacort Asthma Management System

Luxury Homes and Estates

Diary

*National Asthma Education Program, August 1991.

108 BAMFORD AVE.
HAWTHORNE, N.J. 07506

• FAX IN STUDIO •

Frank Riley
ILLUSTRATION

SEE ALSO: AMERICAN SHOWCASE VOL. 7-15.
AND R.S.V.P. VOL. 7-16

• SAMPLES OR PORTFOLIO •
UPON REQUEST

© Frank Riley

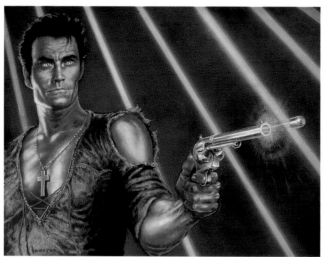

Ned Dameron

P.O. Box 11226
Silver Spring, MD 20913-1226

(301) 585-8512

Classic illustration, competitively priced and evocatively styled, with a versatility that has graced cover and interior illustrations for best selling authors of various genres—ranging from Stephen King to Jennifer Wilde, from Frederick Forsyth to Anne McCaffrey—as well as for magazines, gaming companies, posters, and motion picture productions.
Slides, samples, and client list available upon request.

F O W L E R

I L L U S T R A T I O N S

7 1 7 - 4 8 8 - 5 1 5 1

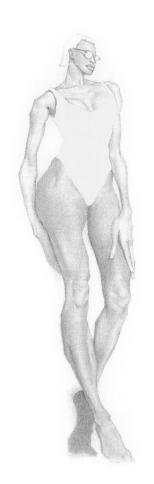

**CARTOON ILLUSTRATION
BY ED KING
717 · 253 · 4104**

GARY OVERACRE

3 8 0 2 V i n e y a r d T r a c e , M a r i e t t a , G e o r g i a 3 0 0 6 2 4 0 4 - 9 7 3 - 8 8 7 8

GARY OVERACRE

3 8 0 2 V i n e y a r d T r a c e , M a r i e t t a , G e o r g i a 3 0 0 6 2 4 0 4 - 9 7 3 - 8 8 7 8

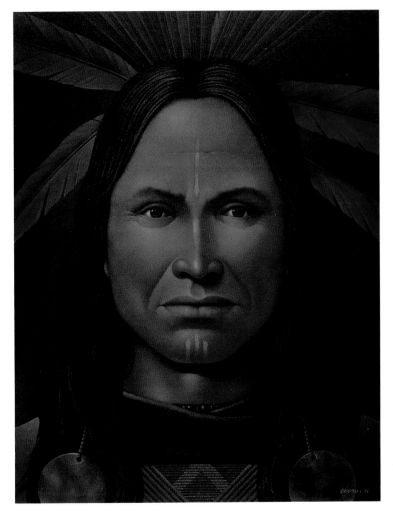

Peter Wallace

43 WACHUSETT STREET
JAMAICA PLAIN, MA 02130

(617) 522-4917

Clients include: *TV Guide, Boston Herald, Bostonia Magazine,* King Features, D.C. Heath, *Kidsports Magazine, Campus Life.*

Cynthia Jabar

326 A STREET
BOSTON, MA 02210

TELEPHONE/FAX
(617) 482-4938

CLIENTS: Andre Deutsch, Boston Globe, Brown Publishing, Candlewick Press, CMC Advertising, Cricket Magazine, David R. Godine Publisher, DC Heath, Ladybug Magazine, Little, Brown and Company, Parents Magazine, Silver Burdett & Ginn.

CHILDRENS BOOKS:
Party Day 1987
Alice Ann Gets Ready For School 1991
Bored Blue? Think What You Can Do 1991
Shimmy Shake Earthquake, Don't Forget To Dance Poems 1992

How Many, How Many, How Many 1993
No Hickory, No Dickory, No Dock—Caribbean Nursery Rhymes 1993

Children's portfolio and samples available upon request.

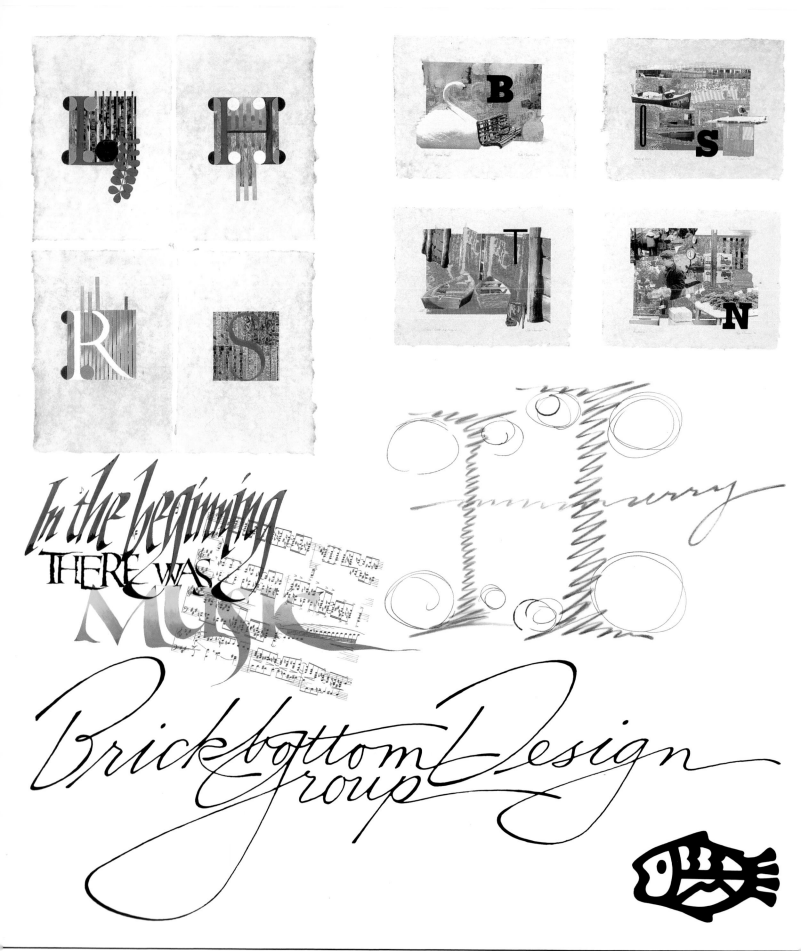

Judith Moncrieff

9 Marina Drive
Spinnaker Island
Hull, MA 02045

(617) 925-5895

Board AIGA Boston Chapter, Graphic
Artist's Guild, Women's Caucus for Art.
Published in American Corporate Iden-
tity, Amiga World, Print Magazine.

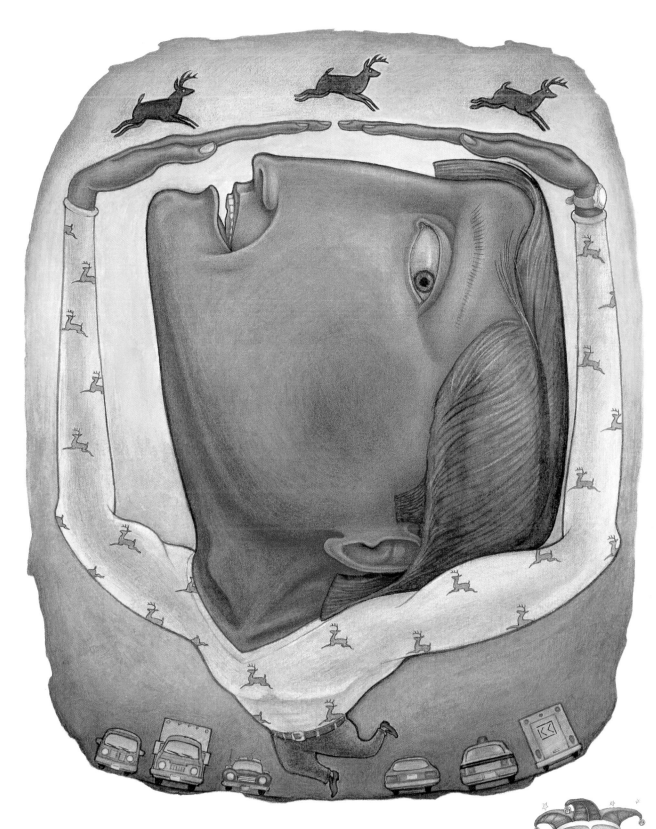

KENT CHRISTENSEN
518 EAST 80TH STREET • NEW YORK, NY 10021 • 212-744-3050

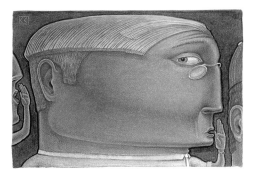

BERLIN
PRODUCTIONS INC

- Illustration for Advertising,
  Children's Books and Editorial
- Character Development
  and Creative Concept
- Computer Illustration and Animation

Rose Mary Berlin • Rick Berlin • Bob Berry

Promotional Innovations/ Sunkist

Connections Unlimited/ Alcone Promotions/ Burger King "Kids Club"

Wetherell Associates/M&M Mars

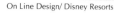

On Line Design/ Disney Resorts

Totonoya Robotics

Additional work can be seen in Showcase 10&14, GAG Directory of Illustration 6 and Adweek Portfolio 88.
Portfolios, reel, and sample self-running computer animation disk are available upon request.

Locke Lane Rd#1 Box 193, Yorktown Heights, New York 10598 Studio/Modem: 914-962-0526, 914-962-0528   Fax: 914-962-2266

PHONE
703 · 532 · 8551

WAYNE VINCENT

FAX
703 · 532 · 1808

To See More Work:

© 1992 Wayne Vincent & Associates
Color Separations by Executive Presentations, Rockville, MD

Showcase 16
Creative Illustration '92

Ben Aronson
33 Wayside Inn Road
Framingham, MA 01701
(508) 788-1455
Fax (508) 877-3734

Clients:
CBS, Epic Records, ITT, Sheraton Corp.,
EG&G, Charrette Corp., Universal
Aluminum Inc., Hansen Lind Meyer,
Trenowth Ltd., Security Computer
Systems Inc., Leaf Systems Inc., Tech
Graphics Inc.

Awards:
1992 Fisher Award, International
ASAP Illustration Competition
1992 Pleissner Award, National
Academy of Design, New York
1990 Schweitzer Award, National
Academy of Design, New York

Member Graphic Artists Guild
© Ben Aronson 1992

©1992 Dave Allen

Dave Allen

MEMBER: Graphic Artists Guild

18108 MARTIN AVE. 2F • HOMEWOOD, IL. 60430
708•798•3283 (FAX IN STUDIO)

National Safety Council

Nation's Business Magazine

National Wildlife Magazine

Maryann Thomas

MARYANN THOMAS ILLUSTRATION
19030 ARCHWOOD STREET #6
RESEDA, CA 91335

PHONE & FAX (818) 705-0289

Clients include: Tyson Chicken, Anheuser-Busch Inc., Tamrac Packs, Combat Pest Control, Leo Burnett Co., Architectural Digest, J&S Floors, Saxon/Ross Film Design, Vinyard National Bank, Raynor Garage Doors, Home Magazine, Sure & Natural, Macmillan Publishing, Houghton Mifflin Company, Teleflora.

My work may also be seen in The Workbook 1987, 1988, 1989 (Vol. 9, 10, 11), American Showcase 1990 (Vol. 4) and Communication Arts Illustration Annual 1989.

Member of the Graphic Artists Guild.

Los Angeles Times

American Airlines

PACE
ILLU
STRA
TION

Clients Include:
American Airlines
Hewlett Packard
Los Angeles Times
Seagrams
Pelican Press
Carolco Pictures
The Wine Enthusiast
TRW
Bank of America

✆ **818 894 6447** CALL FOR FAX NUMBER

MIKE STANFILL
214·320·2293
FAX: 214·321·8680

Plato Taleporos

333 East 23rd Street
New York, NY 10010

(212) 689-3138
Fax in studio

Clients include: Applause Theatre
Books; AdWeek Promote; Audio;
Baltimore Sun; Bozell, Jacobs, Kenyon
& Eckhardt; Business Week; Channels;
Chemical Engineering; Consumer
Reports; Cosmopolitan; Diversion;
Financial World; Governing Magazine;

Harcourt, Brace, Jovanovich; Industry
Week; Kelly Communications; Money
Magazine; New York Life Insurance;
New York Newsday; New York Times;
PC Sources; People Magazine; Private
Clubs; Publishers Weekly; Scholastic;
Ski; Travel & Leisure; US Air; Working

Mother; Workman Press.

Member of the Graphic Artists Guild

James Fogle

ILLUSTRATION

53 PEARL STREET

BROOKLYN, NY 11201

(718) 522-5724

Clients include: Watson Guptill,
Sharp, Mercedes Benz, Pepsi, American
Express, The Energizer, Sears. National
Environmental Education Center,
TBWA, McCaffrey McCall, BBDO.

JOHN C. WARD

125 Maryland Ave. • Freeport, NY 11520 • 516-546-2906

Ami Blackshear

1428 Elm Drive   Novato CA 94945   415•897•9486

S P E E R

ILLUSTRATION

BY

CHRISTOPHER SPEER

Christopher Speer

20130 HATTERAS STREET
WOODLAND HILLS, CA 91367

PHONE & FAX (818) 888-0400

Illustration for Print, TV, and Film
(includes Bugsy, Star Trek VI).
Logo and lettering treatments.

Clients: Disney, MGM, Paramount, Tri
Star Pictures, Tomy Toys, J.C. Penney,
Melrose Clothing, Sebastian and lots of
others you've never heard of.

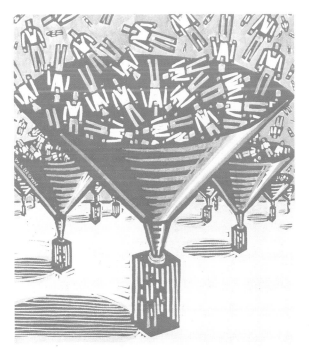

WILLIAM L. BROWN 301·270·2014

William L. Brown

6704 Westmoreland Avenue
Takoma Park, MD 20912

(301) 270-2014 (Voice and Fax)

Dos Equis / Chi Chi's

Blake Thornton

AIRBRUSH AND GRAPHIC ILLUSTRATION

(707) 935-9716

310

Pepsi / Restaurant Manager

IBM / Multimedia Solutions

Sebastiani Vineyards

Beverly Hills 90210 Licensing

© Blake Thornton

Valerie Warren

VALERIE WARREN ILLUSTRATION
14 E. 4TH STREET #1103
NEW YORK, NY 10012

(212) 505-5366

Clients include: Viking Penguin, Simon & Schuster/Pocket Books, MTV, Blue Moon Books, Broadcast Arts, DETAILS, American Health, American Photographer, The Nation, Twilight Zone, Goodtimes/Kids Klassics Video . . .

ANDREA
MISTRETTA

ILLUSTRATION STUDIO

201-652-7531   FAX 652-1294
EST. 1979 • Call me for a free
sample portfolio & client roster.

Anna Veltfort

16 West 86 Street #B
New York, New York 10024

(212) 877-0430

Anne Alden
91 DALE STREET
CHESTNUT HILL, MA 02167

(617) 738-7791

Clients include:
Boston Financial Group
Harvard Business Review
Starlight Foundation
Andrews & McMeel

Member Graphic Artists Guild

TREATNER

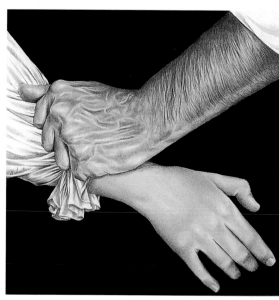

M E R Y L
TREATNER
239 Monroe Street Philadelphia, Pennsylvania 19147 **(215) 627-229**

TREATNER

MERYL
TREATNER
239 Monroe Street Philadelphia, Pennsylvania 19147 (215) 627-2297

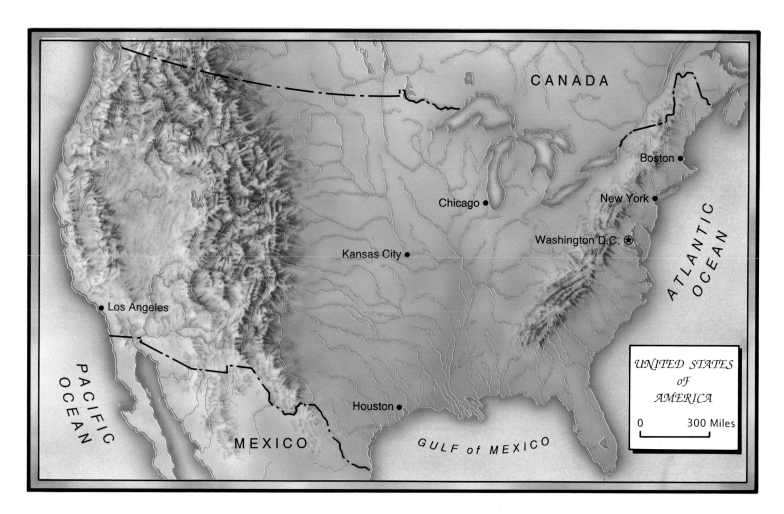

United States of America map

Scale: 0 — 300 Miles

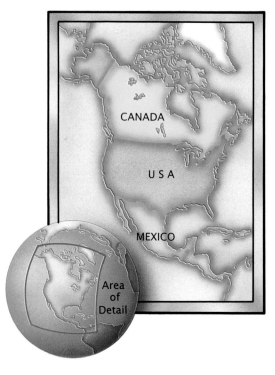

Area of Detail

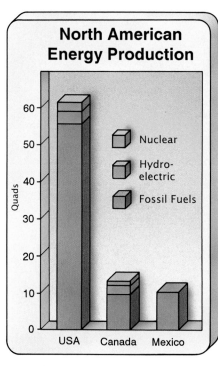

North American Energy Production

Quads

Nuclear
Hydro-electric
Fossil Fuels

USA Canada Mexico

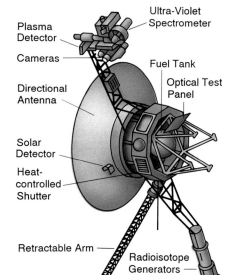

VOYAGER SPACE PROBE

Plasma Detector
Ultra-Violet Spectrometer
Cameras
Fuel Tank
Directional Antenna
Optical Test Panel
Solar Detector
Heat-controlled Shutter
Retractable Arm
Radioisotope Generators

Thomas F. Cranmer

826 Bloomfield Street
Hoboken, NJ 07030

(201) 795-9734

Clients include: Life Magazine
Audubon Magazine
Natural History Magazine
D.C. Heath Publishing
Merrill Lynch
Philip Morris
Mobil Oil

All work available on computer or
by hand.

Natalie Fasolt
165 Avenue A Apt. 9
New York, NY 10009

(212) 473-5909
Fax service available

Graphic Artists Guild Member

Samples sent on request

Clients include: American Express
American Management Association
Boehringer/Mannheim
Dorothy Gray Cosmetics
JC Penney
Levis
Revlon

Kim Wilson Eversz

268 Union Street #3, Brooklyn NY 11231 ☀ 718-237-8546

Shelley Matheis
534 East Passaic Avenue
Bloomfield, New Jersey 07003

(201) 338-9506
Fax (201) 893-1141

Ray J. Goudey II

RAY GOUDEY ILLUSTRATION
1020 CAWSTON AVENUE
SOUTH PASADENA, CA 91030

PHONE: (818) 799-4527
FAX: (818) 441-6047

Shelley Dieterichs

34 N. Gore

Suite 201

Saint Louis

Missouri

63119

PHONE & FAX:

314/ 968-4515

Clients include:

AT&T

General American
Life Insurance

Ralston Purina Company

Hill and Knowlton, Inc.

Mallinckrodt, Inc.

Anheuser-Busch Companies, Inc.

Milliken Publishing

Prentice Hall Publishing

Missouri Botanical Garden

Chris Robertson

3708 Watseka Avenue #216
Los Angeles, CA 90034

(310) 836-8968   Fax available.

Clients include:

Los Angeles Times
Tennis
Playboy
Bicycle Guide
Advertising Age
Sport

Psychology Today
Running Times
Los Angeles Magazine
The Press-Enterprise
Westways
Stocks and Commodities
Entrepreneur

Inside Sports
Movieline
The Walking Magazine
Spin
Sacramento Magazine
California Business
The National Sports Review

D'Ann De La Hoz
(DEH-LAH-ÓZ)
STUDIO D, INC.
7026 SOUTHWEST 106TH PLACE
MIAMI, FLORIDA 33173
☎ (305) 598-7431
FAX (305) 598-3504

Specializing in (bongo roll please…):
Latin, hot, fanny, funny, tropical, salsa,
it's in the jeans, Mambo Kings, you-
know-what-I-mean-kind-a-thing
illustrations.
I CAN BE SERIOUS, TOO.

CLIENTS:
Telemundo TV Network
Spanish Foods, Inc.
The Keyes Company Realtors
Carnival Cruise Lines

MEMBERSHIPS:
Graphic Artists Guild–
Florida Representative
AIGA
©De La Hoz 1992

Larry **NORTON**

I L L U S T R A T I O N

818 797 9837

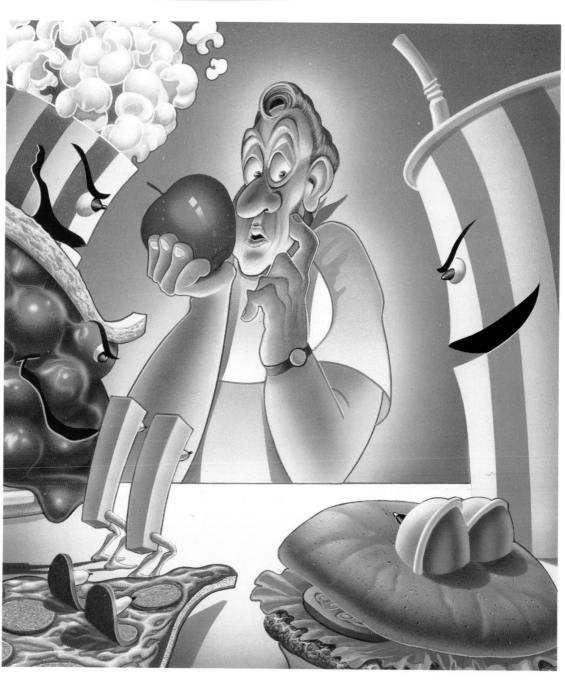

CHANG PARK
52-05 39th RD. #2A
WOODSIDE, N. Y. 11377
(718) 651-3764

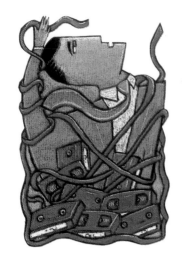

CYNTHIA CARROZZA
ILLUSTRATION

PARTIAL CLIENT LIST: JOHNSON & JOHNSON, FOUR SEASONS HOTEL, HARCOURT   BRACE JOVANOVICH, SIMON & SCHUSTER, HOUGHTON MIFFLIN, CHRISTIAN

16 ASHFORD ST.
BOSTON, MA 02134
617.783.2421
FAX & MODEM:
617.783.0316

CYNTHIA CARROZZA
ILLUSTRATION

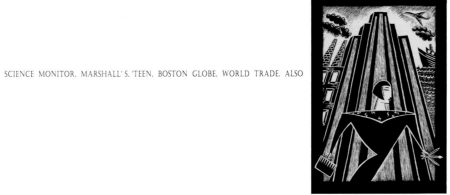

SCIENCE MONITOR, MARSHALL'S, 'TEEN, BOSTON GLOBE, WORLD TRADE. ALSO SEE ADWEEK PORTFOLIOS 1990 AND DIRECTORY OF ILLUSTRATION 8.

16 ASHFORD ST.
BOSTON, MA 02134
617.783.2421
FAX & MODEM:
617.783.0316

Bruce Sereta

11820 Edgewater Drive #315
Lakewood, Ohio 44107

(216) 861-7227

Jeff Yeomans

3838 Kendall Street
San Diego, CA 92109

619/272-8756
619/594-2564

Macintosh® Computer Illustration
capabilities.

Member Society of Illustrators,
Los Angeles.
Member Broadcast Designers'
Association, Inc.

Barclay Shaw

170 East Street
Sharon, CT 06069

phone/fax: 203 • 364 • 5974

Clients include: Accolade, Bantam Doubleday Dell, Baen Books, Berkley Publishing Group, DC Comics, DAW Books, Del Rey Books, Fawcett Books, Field Publishing, Harcourt Brace Jovanovich, Heavy Metal, Macmillan Publishing, Myers Rum, National Audubon Society, OMNI International, Penguin USA, G.P. Putnam's Sons, PBS, Random House, Simon & Schuster, TOR Books, Toys R Us, Time/Warner, Whittle Communications, Ziff-Davis.

Mickey Mouse ©Walt Disney Productions

Frank R. Sofo

16 BRANCH LANE
LEVITTOWN, NY 11756

(516) 681-8745 OR
(212) 459-5255

Clients include:
BBDO
Jordan, McGrath, Case & Taylor Inc.
N.W. Ayer
J. Walter Thompson
Doubleday Book & Music Clubs Inc.

MICHAEL
THORNTON

Michael Thornton

7844 Starward Drive
Dublin, CA 94568

(510) 828-5032
Fax in studio

KEN JOUDREY

REPRESENTED BY DAY YANTIS, PHONE & FAX (203) 378-5007

T. Kennedy

Layout / Design / Illustration
Represented by: Clients' Choice

812-853-2911
FAX 812-853-0575

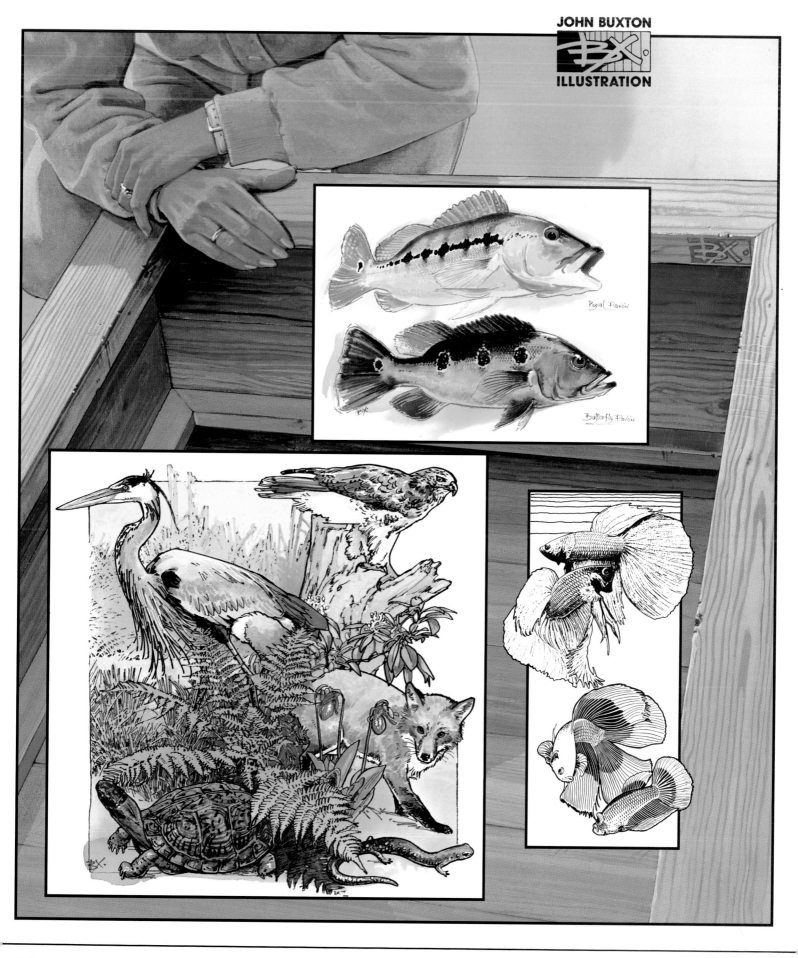

John Buxton

4584 Sylvan Drive
Allison Park, PA 15101

Phone & Fax (412) 486-6588

The above illustrations were completed for: American Kennel Club, *Flyfishing Magazine,* National Geographic Society, and the International Betta Congress.

Other recent clients: Alcoa, Copperweld, PPG, Penn Southwest, Servicestar Hardware, Pat Transit Authority, Bradbury Press, *Golf Illustrated Magazine,* Frontiers International, and Humana. Portfolio available.

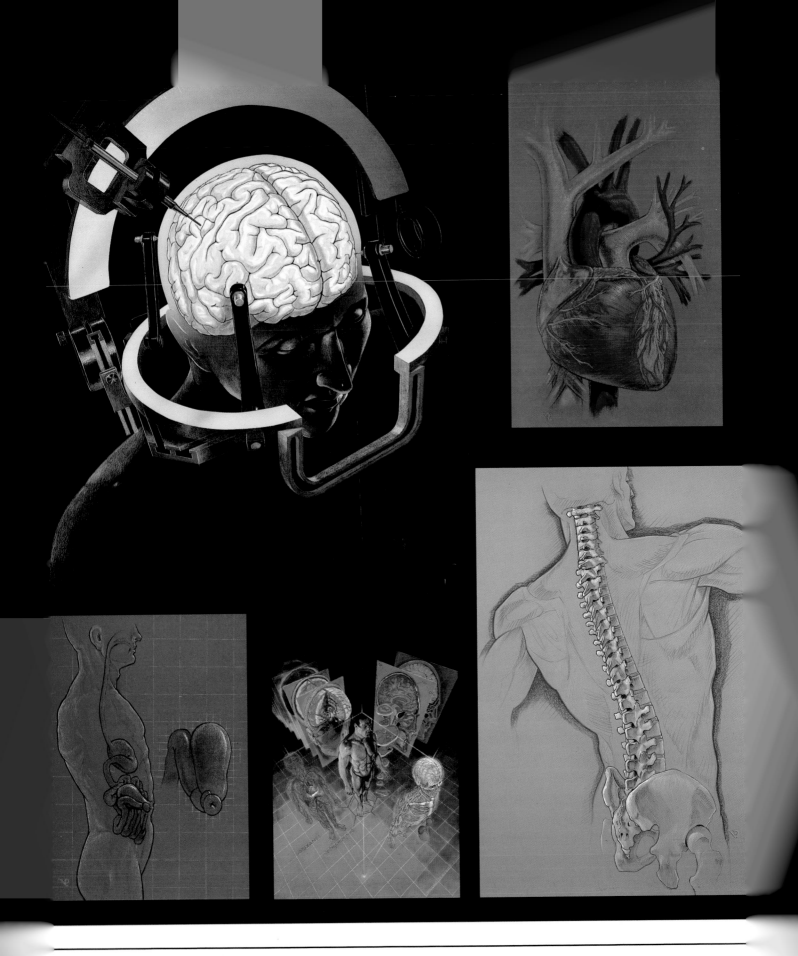

cent Perez Studio

WEBER STREET
DA, CALIFORNIA 94501

521-2262
10) 522-2300

Medical, Editorial, and Fantasy
Illustration
Paintings, Drawings, Pop-Ups and
Woodcuts

Member GAG, SISF, AMI

Partial client list: *Time* Magazine, *Play-*
boy, Lucasfilm, ABC TV, Disney, Syntex,
Immunex, National Medical Enter-
prises, Seton Medical Center, Cutter
Labs, Hewlett Packard, Hana Biologics,
Ciba-Geigy.
See also American Showcase 9, 10, 11,
12; Bay Area Creative Sourcebook 1 & 2;

Workbook 12; Creative Illustratio
Medical Illustration Sourcebook

Awards (partial list)
Gold—RX Club, Western Art Dir
Club; Excellence—CA Design Ar
LULU; Merit—SINY, AIGA, SILA

Marilynn Grant Barr
9 1 9 / 8 5 2 - 4 2 8 7 • F A X - 9 1 9 / 8 5 2 - 8 7 7 5

Marilynn Grant Barr
5721 Wildberry Drive
Greensboro, North Carolina 27409

919/852-4287 • Fax 919/852-8775

Lane Gregory

Represented by Gwen Walters Goldstein
50 Fuller Brook Rd. • Wellesley, MA 02181 • 617-235-8658

Susan Spellman

Represented by Gwen Walters Goldstein
50 Fuller Brook Rd. • Wellesley, MA 02181 • 617-235-8658

Gwen Walters Goldstein represents professional illustrators catering to the needs of advertising and book publishing. Call today to receive a complete listing of illustrators and the wide variety of styles from cartoon to photo realism offered to handle your special needs. Fax available.

Kathleen O'Malley

Represented by Gwen Walters Goldstein
50 Fuller Brook Rd. • Wellesley, MA 02181 • 617-235-8658

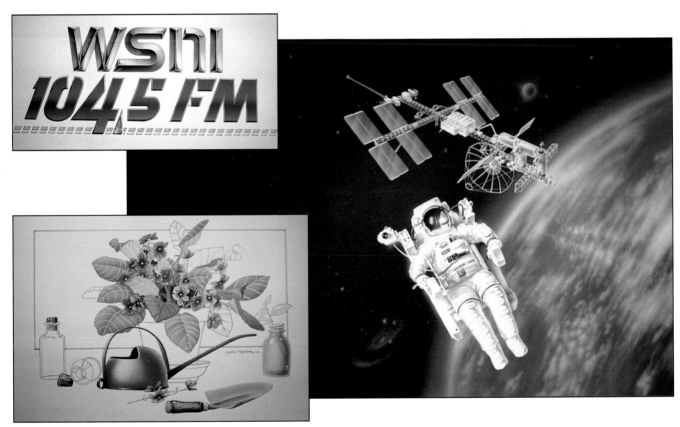

Gary Torrisi

Represented by Gwen Walters Goldstein
50 Fuller Brook Rd. • Wellesley, MA 02181 • 617-235-8658

Gwen Walters Goldstein represents professional illustrators catering to the needs of advertising and book publishing. Call today to receive a complete listing of illustrators and the wide variety of styles from cartoon to photo realism offered to handle your special needs. Fax available.

Nan Rossiter

ILLUSTRATOR
14 PLEASANT STREET
NEW MILFORD, CT 06776

(203) 354-3065

Sporting News Mag.

FlexLite Inc.

Information Week

JACK MOORE STUDIO

Please call for your free mini-portfolio.
201/627-6931 · FAX 625-4179

Dick Cole
414 Jackson Street, Suite 204
San Francisco, CA

(415) 986-8163
Fax (415) 421-1135

Represented by:
Pamela Peek and Ann Koeffler
(213) 957-2327
Fax (213) 957-1910

Watercolorist: Subject matter ranges
from Aardvark to Zweiback and just
about everything else in between.

ILLUSTRATION IN BLACK & WHITE AND COLOR

CYNTHIA BUSCH

718 383 3160

Death By Chocolate, Kenan Books

Without You, I'm Dragon! Greeting Card

November 91 Readers' Survey, Ladies Home Journal

978 LORIMER STREET • BROOKLYN NY 11222

FAX IN STUDIO • TO VIEW MORE WORK, SEE GAG DIRECTORY #7

Samples available
for viewing at:

Leo Art Studio

276 Fifth Avenue
New York, N.Y. 10001
(212) 685-3174

Clients Include
Susan Crane
American Greetings
Augus Communications
C.R. Gibson
Hallmark Cards
Marcel Schurman

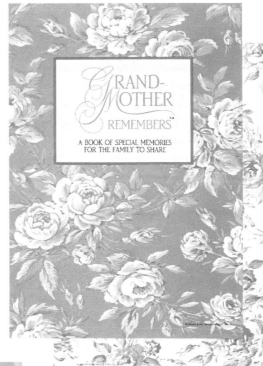

GRAND-MOTHER REMEMBERS™

A BOOK OF SPECIAL MEMORIES
FOR THE FAMILY TO SHARE

Kumiko Robinson
4667 Country Creek Dr., #1162
Dallas, Texas 75236
(214) 337-0562

349

Craig Yoe + Janet Morra-Yoe

YOE-YOE STUDIO
INCORPORATED
NEW YORK
TEL 914·271·5035
FAX 914·271·9721

Artists Interpret The World's Favorite Mouse

THE ART OF
MICKEY MOUSE

JOHN UPDIKE

Edited by
CRAIG YOE and JANET MORRA YOE

WHAT WE DO

▶ Animation
▶ Toy Design
▶ Package Design
▶ Premium Design
▶ Marketing, Advertising + Promotion Ideas
▶ Logos + Lettering
▶ Book Packaging

▶ Illustration
▶ Product Styling
▶ Licensing Design + Art
▶ Character Design
▶ Theme Park Design
▶ Textile + Apparel Design
▶ Consultation

WHO WE'VE DONE IT FOR

▶ Nickelodeon
▶ MTV
▶ The Walt Disney Co.
▶ Mattel, Inc.
▶ Parker Brothers
▶ McDonald's
▶ BBDO
▶ Jim Henson's Muppets
▶ Davidson Marketing
▶ Pomposello Productions
▶ Kellogg's
▶ Ryan Partnership
▶ Pizza Hut
▶ Kraft/General Foods
▶ Fascinations Toys
▶ Hart Enterprises, Inc.
▶ Wendy's
▶ The Smithsonian
▶ Helm Products, Ltd.
▶ J.J. Sedelmaier Productions
▶ Sesame Street
▶ Marvel Comics
▶ Topps
▶ ABC Records
▶ Broadcast Arts
▶ D.C. Comics
▶ Burger King
▶ Capri Sun
▶ Hyperion
▶ CBS
▶ IBM
▶ NBA
▶ NBC

©1992 Yoe-Yoe Studio Incorporated.

Janet Morra-Yoe + Craig Yoe

YOE-YOE STUDIO
INCORPORATED
NEW YORK
TEL 914·271·5035
FAX 914·271·9721

FREE

▶ A set of **8** collectable, limited edition, trading cards
to you when you order and mention this ad!

THE
DARK ANGEL

PIERS ANTHONY

UNIVERSITY

Briar Lee Mitchell, M.A.

6749 Babcock Avenue
North Hollywood, CA 91606

(818) 982-8594
Fax (818) 982-4189

Clients include:
Lucasfilms, Ltd.
Banana Road Productions
The Smithsonian
Disney

GINA HENDRIX

PH/FAX (816) 931-8267 3921 WARWICK, K.C.,MO. 64111

"I see you have connections with the spirit world."

WINNER OF "THE ABSOLUT® CARTOON CONTEST"

ABSOLUT GOMEZ.

LORETTA GOMEZ

PHONE: 201·656·5329 HOBOKEN, N.J. FAX: 201·653·1923

Discover Cable's Treasures

CATHY MORRISON

BIG CHIEF GRAPHICS

775 EAST PANAMA DRIVE

LITTLETON, CO 80121

303 798-0424

FAX 303 797-1403

VOICE ▶ 617·524·3099 • FAX ▶ 617·524·5151

All It Takes Is Imagination.

Yours and Mine.

If you have any questions,
or would like additional
samples, please call.
Thank you.

David Lesh

317.253.3141

FAX 317.255.8462

Represented in the East
by Joanne Palulian
1.203.866.3734
1.212.581.8338

THE AEON GROUP / 800•835•1949

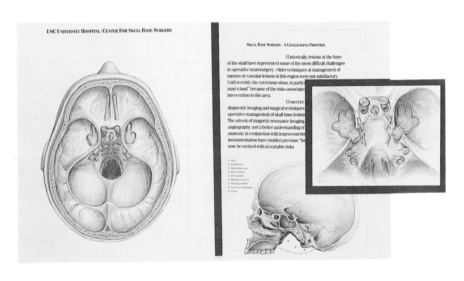

KERNE ERICKSON

714•364•1141
800•835•1949

Mary Louise Pierson

Mary Louise Pierson
RR 1 Box 68B
THETFORD CENTER, VERMONT 05075

(802) 333-9996

Member of Graphic Artists Guild
© Mary Louise Pierson 1992

Peter Bono
908·496·8524
Fax 908·496·8724
63 Stark Road   Columbia NJ 07832

I can originate concepts or work with your design. I exhibited at the Society of Illustrators, NYC. I have worked for everybody.

Frank Zappa

Left:
Ted Kennedy

Right:
Larry King

Gary Hovland

3408 Crest Drive
Manhattan Beach, CA 90266

(310) 545-6808
Fax (310) 546-1386

Clients include: Conde Nast Traveler, The New York Times magazine, Business Week, Newsweek, Time, Sports Illustrated, Money, The Los Angeles Times, The Washington Post, The American Express Corporation, Ogilvy & Mather Advertising, Grey Advertising, Leo Burnett Advertising, and Alfred Knopf Publishing.

Gary Hovland

3408 Crest Drive
Manhattan Beach, CA 90266

(310) 545-6808
Fax (310) 546-1386

Clients include: Conde Nast Traveler, The New York Times magazine, Business Week, Newsweek, Time, Sports Illustrated, Money, The Los Angeles Times, The Washington Post, The American Express Corporation, Ogilvy & Mather Advertising, Grey Advertising, Leo Burnett Advertising, and Alfred Knopf Publishing.

Ken Coffelt

illustrator

Los Angeles

California

818 l 884 - 4274

Fax: 818 l 884 - 3937

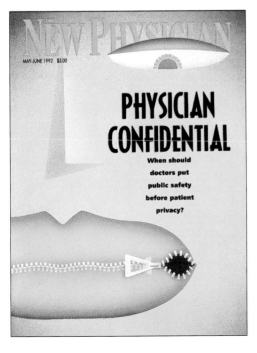

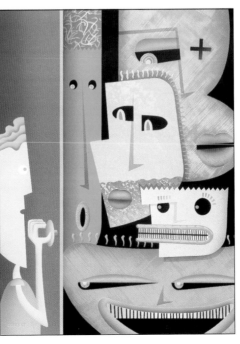

◄ IBM

ALL ILLUSTRATIONS AND CHARACTER DESIGNS © DANIELLE JONES 1993

▲ EN ROUTE MAGAZINE

◄ READER'S DIGEST

BLUE MOUNTAIN ►

▼ ONTARIO HYDRO

D A N I E L L E

JONES

416·968·6277

Illustration of a Humorous Nature

ALL ILLUSTRATIONS AND CHARACTER DESIGNS © DANIELLE JONES 1993

▲ TORONTO STOCK EXCHANGE

▲ STAR-KIST PET FOODS

D A N I E L L E
JONES
416·968·6277

Illustration of a Humorous Nature

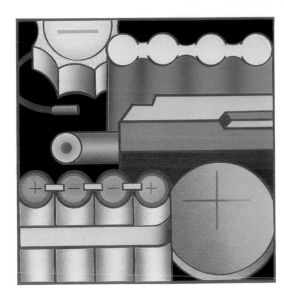

Annie Gusman

15 King Street
Putnam, CT 06260

(203) 928-1042
Fax (203) 928-1238

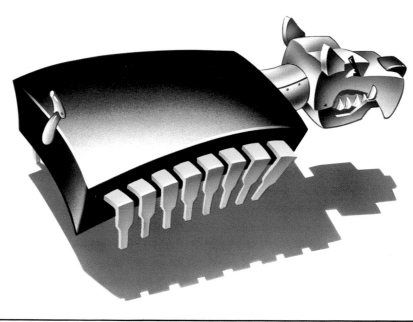
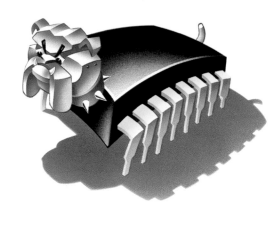

Dave Joly
15 KING STREET
PUTNAM, CT 06260

(203) 928-1042
FAX (203) 928-1238

Stan Gorman

STAN GORMAN ART COMMUNICATIONS
185 ESPLANADE
IRVINE, CA 92715

(714) 733-8071
FAX IN STUDIO.

Clients include: Applause, Inc.; Asher Gould Advertising; Avery Label Co.; Bermudez & Assoc.; Carnation Foods; Deutsch Shea & Evans; Disneyland; Grey Advertising; Kaiser, McEuen Inc.; Ketchum, Bohle Advertising; Kresser, Craig/D.I.K.; Jacques Cousteau Ocean Center; J.D. Powers & Assoc.; J. Walter Thompson Advertising; L.A. Gear; Litton Data Systems; Lockheed Aviation; Los Angeles RTD; Macmillan/McGraw-Hill; Marvel Productions; MCA; McCann-Erickson; MPI-A.A.R.P.; Nationwide Advertising; Ogilvy & Mather/ West; Pennsylvania Life; Persechini & Co.; Prime Ticket; Toyota; 20th Century Fox; United Cable Television.

Margery Mintz
9 COTTAGE AVENUE
SOMERVILLE, MA 02144

(617) 623-2291

Clients include: Digital, AT&T, State
Street Bank, Kodak, New England
Telephone, Fleet Bank, Holiday Inn,
Houghton-Mifflin, Polaroid.

STEPHEN
JOHNSON

81 Remsen Street ▼ Apt.1 ▼ Brooklyn ▼ New York ▼ 11201 ▼ 718/237-2352

STEPHEN
JOHNSON

81 Remsen Street ▾ Apt.1 ▾ Brooklyn ▾ New York ▾ 11201 ▾ 718/237-2352

© NFL Properties, Inc.

Alain Moreau

PAINTER/ILLUSTRATOR
1844 SWEET BRIAR PL.
THOUSAND OAKS, CA 91362

(805) 493-0650

ABC Records, Paramount Records,
United Artists Records, Warner
Brothers Records, Dell Publishing,
Universal Pictures, 20th Century Fox,
Carnation Co., Serono Labs, GTE,
National Football League, Georgetown
Television Productions, Peppertree
Ranch Art Show, Arts For The Parks.

Tom Durfee

414 JACKSON STREET
SAN FRANCISCO, CA 94111

(415) 781-0527

I've been an illustrator for the past 18 years and have spent equal time as an agency art director—making me well acquainted with the conceptual and visual challenges in advertising and how to resolve them. You'll find my portfolio reflects more of the humorous side of life, but I also work with serious subjects. My work ranges from black and white to full color— including editorial and book illustration. Also available is an animated TV spot created for Dean Witter in which I developed the style and character.

Other clients include British Petroleum and the Australian Tourist Commission.

ERIC VON SCHMIDT

818·559·1490

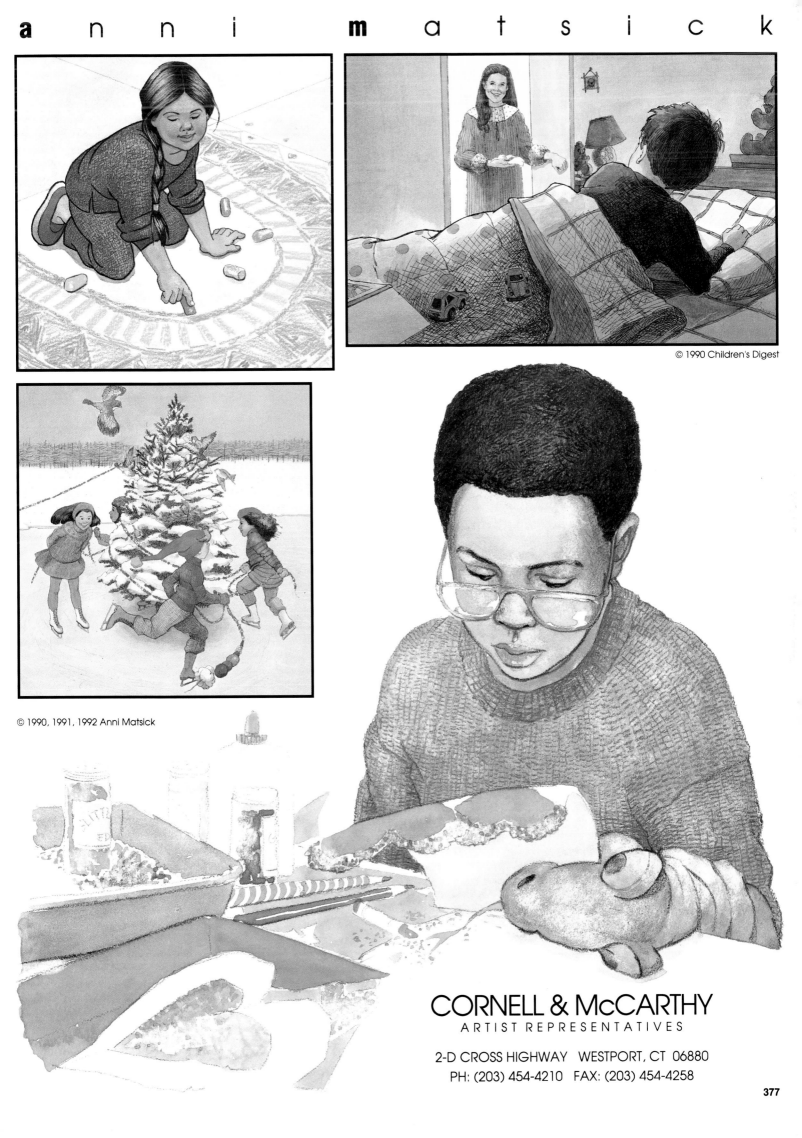

anni matsick

© 1990 Children's Digest

© 1990, 1991, 1992 Anni Matsick

CORNELL & McCARTHY
ARTIST REPRESENTATIVES

2-D CROSS HIGHWAY   WESTPORT, CT 06880
PH: (203) 454-4210   FAX: (203) 454-4258

I HAVE AN IDEA...

James Bond shoes

Hunting tool

Burglar's friend

Amazing Circus act

Roach torture

Cherry skewer

Bubble maker

South-of-the-border bedding

No-nonsense eyewear

Fashion statement

Cob lifter

Anger venter

Dissecting tool

Laura Cornell
118 EAST 93RD STREET, APT. 1A
NEW YORK, NY 10128

(212) 534-0596

Loyal rent-paying clients have included: Forbes magazine, Family Circle, Health, New York magazine, New York Times, New Woman, Seventeen, Sports Illustrated, Working Mother, Harper Collins (Annie Bananie, Earl's Too Cool for Me, Leonora O'Grady).

Other clients have included: Denver Art Museum, Price Waterhouse, TRW, Dial Publishing, D.C. Heath, Houghton Mifflin, Macmillan.

Member Graphic Artists Guild.

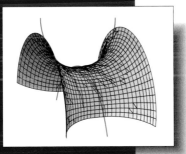

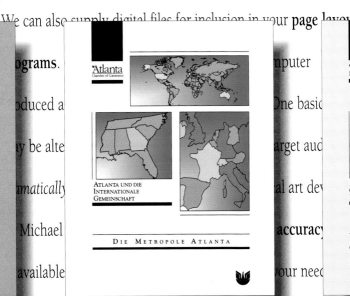

The goal is simple. *Provide our clients with the highest quality art possible*. Whatever your needs, Michael Morrow Art & Design is prepared to deliver… on schedule. Final art may be delivered in a variety of formats including imagesetter film and 35mm slides. We can also supply digital files for inclusion in your **page layout programs**. computer produced a One basic may be alte target aud matically al art dev Michael **accuracy** available our need range from medical to mathematical, Michael Morrow Art & Design is ready. Need special characters or icons for your publication? Want a special math script for your next textbook? No problem. We can build Postscript® fonts to your specification Art that was once sent out for airbrushing can now be delivered complete saving days and even weeks in total production time. You don't need technical art? **Fine**. Michael Morrow Art & Design can deliver. Editorial or incidental art? 3D renderings? Photorealistic animation? Something in-between? **Call**. Michael Morrow Art & Design has the talent and experience to meet your needs. We combine old world skills with new age technology *to provide our clients with the highest quality art possible*.

MICHAEL MORROW
a r t   &   d e s i g n

800.377.4080   404.949.2745   fax: 404.949.7691

ostscript is a registered trademark of Adobe Systems, Inc.

GARNET HENDERSON • 820 HUDSON STREET • HOBOKEN, NEW JERSEY 07030 • 201 653 3948

GARNET HENDERSON • 820 HUDSON STREET • HOBOKEN, NEW JERSEY 07030 • 201 653 3948

©1992 Bruce Wolfe Ltd

"This campaign is from the self-fulfilling-prophecy-school of advertising. Art Director John Robert Evans and I wanted to demonstrate Kawasaki's unique connection with the people who know and ride motorcycles by telling their stories at the places they gathered together.

But we needed a twist, something to make it special.

So we came up with a series of stories about what might happen to a Kawasaki rider at a certain place on a certain day, in the future.

Alice's Restaurant
Skyline Boulevard
Woodside, California
June 8, 1989

You tighten the chin strap, turn the key, hit the button and the engine snaps to attention like a West Point cadet. You ease the big bike out of the dark garage into the too bright Northern California sunshine.

The Ninja® idles its way through the early morning traffic as you get reacquainted after the week's layoff. The last sleepy faced driver grows small in your mirrors, then disappears as the road opens up and snakes out ahead.

As the twists and bends come closer together, so do you and the machine. You can sense the engineering at work, but feel it only as smooth, balanced performance. Each twist of the throttle reels in the next corner, each squeeze of the brakes sets you up for the next quick shift.

A sweeping left, a little jog to the right and you pull into the carnival that is an Alice's Sunday morning. Time to eat and stretch and talk about how good it was and how great it's gonna be. The bike ticks a little as it begins to cool off. You don't tick, but you could stand to cool down a little yourself.

Some days, life is truly good. Other days, it's even better.

Kawasaki
Let the good times roll.

Remember riding safe is riding smart. Always wear a helmet, eye protection and proper apparel. Passengers, too. Ride defensively. Obey the basic speed law. Never ride under the influence of drugs or alcohol. Adhere to the maintenance schedule in your Owner's Manual. Call 1-800-447-4700 for the Motorcycle Safety Foundation beginner or expert course near you. You do not need a motorcycle to take the course. Specifications and price subject to change without notice. Availability may be limited.

Now if you're an Art Director (and you've actually read this far) ask yourself this; who would you choose other than Bruce Wolfe to bring this idea to life?

See? We were stuck with each other.

And Bruce's paintings didn't just illustrate events, they helped create them.

So how did it all work out?

The campaign won awards. Kawasaki sold motorcycles.

The leading motorcycle magazine named the advertising 'Campaign of the Decade,' and not because we bought the most ads. And 10,000 people showed up in a pouring rain for the first event. You couldn't get that many motorcyclists together in one place if you gave away free beer.

Some fun. We'll have to do it again sometime."

– Scott Young, Creative Director
Evans, Hardy and Young

Representatives:

Debra Weiss
1123 ½ N. Sweetzer Ave
Los Angeles, CA 90069
213 656 5029

Joel Harlib Assoc.
405 N. Wabash
Chicago, IL 60611
312 329 1370

Ron Sweet
716 Montgomery
San Francisco, CA 94111
415 433 1222

Vicki Morgan
194 Third Ave.
New York, NY 10003
212 475 0440

Woody Coleman Presents
490 Rockside Rd.
Cleveland, OH 44131
216 661 4222

Bruce Wolfe Studio
206 El Cerrito Ave.
Piedmont, CA 94611
510 655 7871
FAX 601 7200

cunctation – *delay, tardiness, procrastination.*

epexegesis – *the addition of a word or sentence to explain preceding words, phrases and sentences.*

PICTURES FOR ANY WORDS
FRANK COLLYER
PHONE OR FAX:
914·947·3050

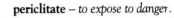

obfuscate – *to confuse, bewilder, or stupefy.*

periclitate – *to expose to danger.*

Frank Collyer

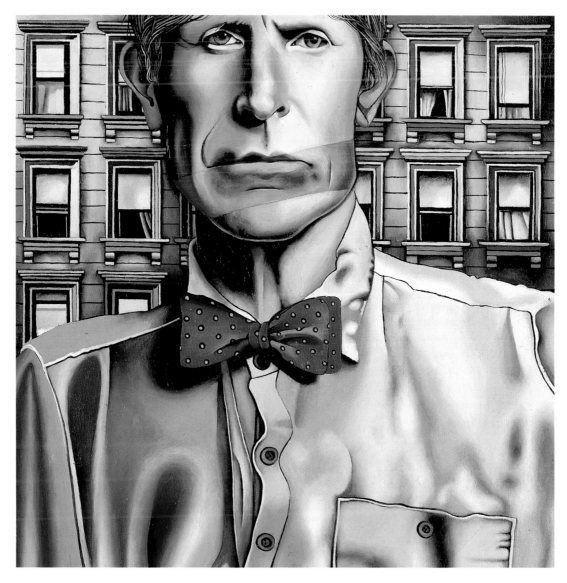

Jeff Hoppa
21-54 Crescent Street, A-8
Long Island City, NY 11105

Phone/Fax (718) 777-1292

Clients include: *The Boston Globe, Forbes, Governing, L.A. Style, Manhattan, Inc., Musician, The New York Daily News, New York Woman, Pittsburgh, The Plain Dealer, Psychology Today, USA Weekend, The Village Voice, The Washington Post.*

Member Graphic Artists Guild
All illustrations © Jeff Hoppa.

VIEW FROM MY WINDOWS IN SPRING

Claude Martinot

145 2 Avenue
New York, NY 10003
(212) 473-3137
Studio: 1133 Broadway, Suite 1614
New York, NY 10010
(212) 645-0097   Fax: (212) 691-3657

A partial list of of my clients: The
Bronx Zoo, Brooklyn Botanic Garden,
Chase Manhattan Bank, D.C. Heath,
Macmillan/McGraw-Hill, Newbridge
Communications, Scholastic.

Samples of my work can be seen in
American Showcase 16, The Creative
Illustration Book 1992, 1993, The GAG
Directory of Illustration 7, 8, 9, RSVP
16, 17, 18.

©Claude Martinot
Member of the Graphic Artists Guild

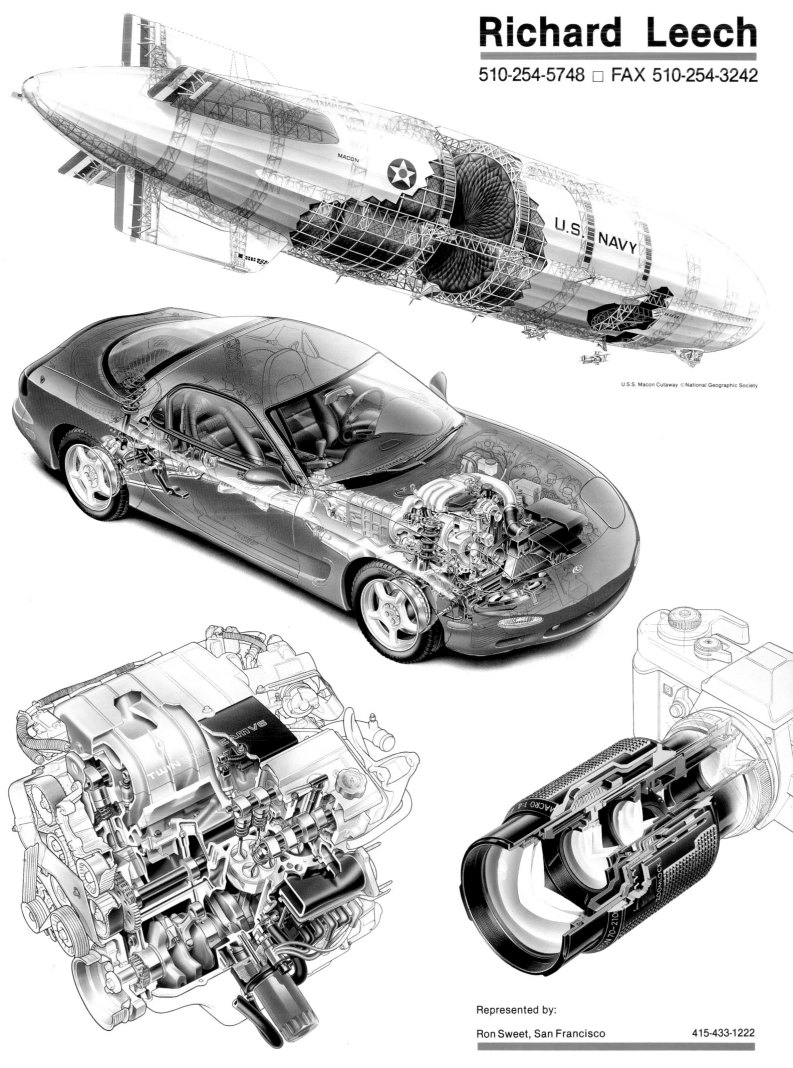

Richard Leech

510-254-5748 ☐ FAX 510-254-3242

U.S.S. Macon Cutaway ©National Geographic Society

Represented by:

Ron Sweet, San Francisco   415-433-1222

Mary O'Keefe Young

62 MIDCHESTER AVENUE
WHITE PLAINS, NY 10606

(914) 949-0147

Additional work may be seen in
American Showcase #12, #13, #14
and Directory of Illustration #8
Member Graphic Artists Guild
Watercolor and Pastel Illustrations.

Clients include: Abbott Labs, Allison
Greetings, Atheneum, Bozell Inc., Cas-
well Massey, C.R. Gibson, Country
Journal, Crown, Dodd Mead, Easter
Seals, Harcourt Brace Jovanovich,
Macmillan, MBI Inc., Ottenheimer,

Readers Digest, Scholastic, Simon and
Schuster, Thomas Nelson Australia.

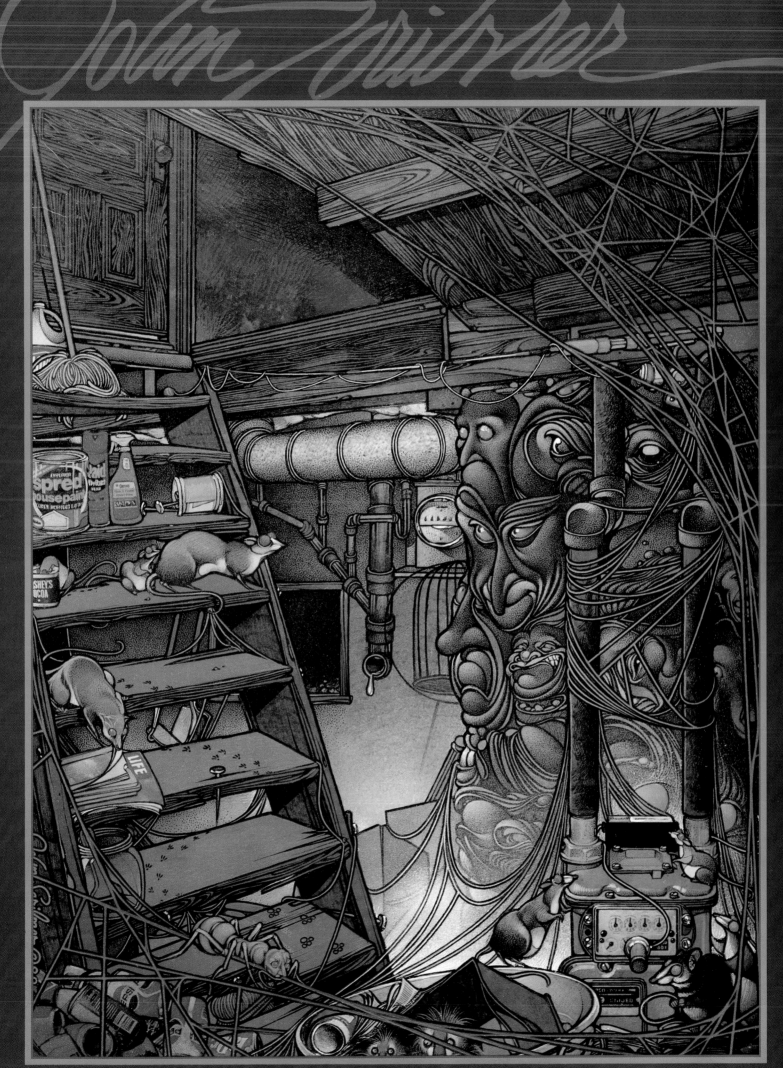

JOANNE SCRIBNER 3314 N LEE, SPOKANE WA 99207 (509) 484-3208

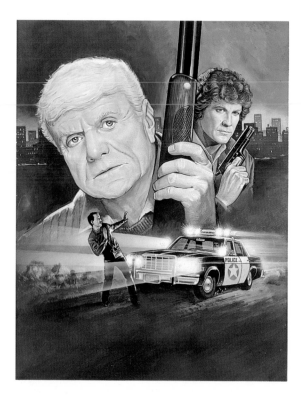  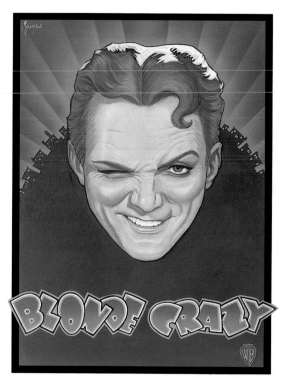

Greg Theakston

PURE IMAGINATION
88 LEXINGTON AVENUE
NEW YORK, NY 10016

(212) 686-0652
FAX (212) 683-3664

Greg Theakston has been illustrating books and magazines for twenty years. Client: National Lampoon, ABC Television, CBS Television, Rolling Stone, DC Comics, Marvel Comics, SFM Media Corporation, Mad Magazine, Miramax Films, and numerous paperback and periodical publishers.

Illustration Guide: Top row: New Kids On The Block as The Simpsons for *Mad Magazine*. Second row: *Hardcastle and McCormick* for ABC Television; Sinatra for Jass Records; Madonna for Personality; James Cagney for self-promotion. Row three: *Rotten to the Core* NYC politicians for Eclipse Products; *Jungle Book* for SFM Media Corp. All images © Theakston.

HIGH PRESSURE DEADLINES ARE OUR SPECIALTY.

Peggi Roberts
ROBERTS ILLUSTRATION
13075 N. 75TH PLACE
SCOTTSDALE, AZ 85260

(602) 991-8568   (602) 998-8152

Represented by:
Bernstein & Andriulli Inc.
(212) 682-1490
Hall & Associates (310) 652-7322

Color portfolio available on request.

Client list: *First* Magazine, *Woman's World* Magazine, U-Haul, Campbell's, America West Airlines, Pepsi, Madison Publishing, Silver Burdett & Ginn, Macmillan/McGraw-Hill, MCA Records, Charles Schwab Investments, Honda, First Interstate Bank, Dillard's, Mayo Clinic, Arizona Lottery.

James Swanson (708) 383-0141 Fax (708) 445-0533

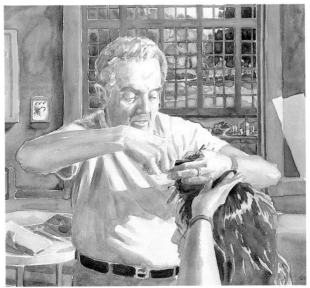

Dana Schreiber

36 CENTER STREET
COLLINSVILLE, CT 06022-1160

(203) 693-6688
FAX (203) 693-6444

© 1992 DANA SCHREIBER

Clients include: Borden, Brooklyn Botanic Garden, Brooklyn Museum, CIGNA, Citibank, Cronin Adv., Doug Cramer Productions, Deare Marketing, Design 5, Emery Adv., Eureka/Regina, First Magazine, Group Four Design, Horizon Software, Lomonaco Design, The Institute of Living, ITT/Hartford, Keiler Adv., Konica, Maier Adv., Moss Warner Design, Neil Davis Design, NBC, Pratt Institute, RKO General, Savin Communications, Scholastic Pub., Signature Marketing, Silver, Burdett & Ginn Pub., Skidmore, Owens & Merrill, Solar Vision Pub., Trumph

Member: Graphic Artists Guild, Society of Illustrators

Charleston

© 1992 Yvonne Buchanan

Yvonne Buchanan
18 Lincoln Place #2L
Brooklyn, NY 11217

718.783.6682
718.622.4094 Fax

Mini-portfolio available upon request.

HEATHER·KING
707·226·1232

· architecture · animals · botanicals · children · florals · food ·
· interiors · landscapes · portraits · products · still life · in watercolor ·

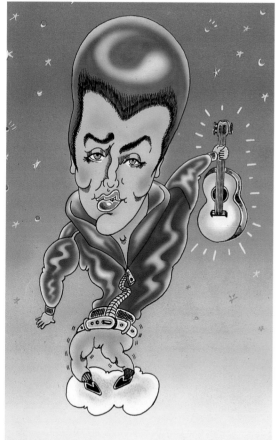

Sally Pogwizd

ASTRO GRAPHICS
124 N. PARK STREET
WESTMONT, IL 60559
(708) 969-5854
FAX (708) 969-5879

Clients have included Kraft General Foods, Leaf, Inc., National Safety Council, U.S. Gypsum, Playboy Magazine, The Market Place Food Store, Recycled Paper Products Greeting Cards, Columbia Audio/Video, Santa Monica Hospital Birth Place, Inside Chicago Magazine.

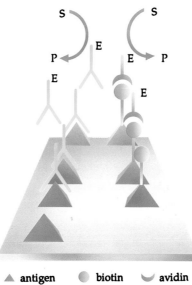

▲ antigen   ● biotin   ◡ avidin

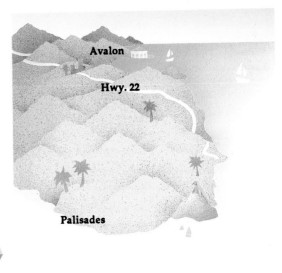

Karen Minot

1-800-257-7103

Specializing in maps and charts.

Client list includes: American Red Cross, Bank of America, BioRad, Levi Strauss, McGraw-Hill Publishing, Metropolitan Transportation Commission of California, Pacific Gas and Electric,

Rodale Press, Thermo Electron Technologies, Travel Holiday, Van Nostrand/Reinhold.

Member Society of Illustrators, San Francisco.

Marie Masciovecchio
90 Gold Street #3J
New York, NY 10038

(212) 233-3672
Fax available

Member of Graphic Artists Guild

Fine art for individual and corporate
clients. Advertising and all medias.

Mehosh

Hand Painted Photography

1016 OLIVE STREET • SANTA BARBARA • CALIFORNIA • 93101 • 805 • 966 • 2332 / 683 • 0404

Mehosh

© MEHOSH

Hand Painted Photography

1016 OLIVE STREET • SANTA BARBARA • CALIFORNIA • 93101 • 805 • 966 • 2332 / 683 • 0404